On the Shores
of Politics

◆————————

JACQUES RANCIÈRE

Translated
by Liz Heron

VERSO

London • New York

This book has been published with financial support from the French Ministry of Culture.

First published by Verso 1995
This edition © Verso 1995
Translation © Liz Heron 1995
First published as *Aux bords du politique*
© Editions Osiris 1992

Verso
UK: 6 Meard Street, London W1V 3HR
USA: 180 Varick Street, New York NY 10014–4606

Verso is the imprint of New Left Books

ISBN 0–86091–467–4
ISBN 0–86091–637–5 (pbk)

British Library Cataloguing in Publication Data
A catalogue record for this book is available from the
British Library

Library of Congress Cataloging-in-Publication Data
Rancière, Jacques.
 [Aux bords du politique.   English]
 On the shores of politics / Jacques Rancière : translated by
Liz Heron.
   p.   cm. — (Phronesis)
 Includes bibliographical references.
 ISBN 0–86091–467–4 (hbk). — ISBN 0–86091–637–5 (pbk)
 1. Democracy. 2. Post-communism. I. Title. II. Series:
Phronesis (London, England)
JC423.R27813   1995
320.9′009′049—dc20   95–18841
                                                                          CIP

Typeset by M Rules
Printed and bound in Great Britain by
Biddles Ltd, Guildford and King's Lynn

Contents

Acknowledgements

'The End of Politics' is based on a paper presented to the Franco-Brazilian symposium on 'Power' held on 9, 10 and 11 May 1988 at the Collège International de Philosophie, on the invitation of Pierre-Jean Labarrière. The text was subsequently reworked to be given as a paper to the philosophy departments of Edinburgh University and Essex University in February 1989.

'The Uses of Democracy' was the topic of a paper for the symposium 'Democracia, democracia social y participación' organized in Santiago de Chile by the Centro de Estudios de la realidad contemporánea in December 1986. An early version was published in Spanish in *Democracia y participación*, edited by Rodrigo Alvayay and Carlos Ruiz (CERC, Santiago, 1988).

'The Community of Equals' is based on a lecture given at the invitation of Miguel Abensour in a discussion forum with Alain Badiou at the Collège International de Philosophie, on 11 May 1987.

'Democracy Corrected' was originally published in *Le genre humain*, no. 22, Autumn 1990.

Translator's Acknowledgement

I wish to thank Donald Nicholson-Smith for his generous and invaluable help with this translation.

Introduction

To speak of the boundaries of the political realm would seem to evoke no precise or current reality. Yet legend invariably has the political begin at one boundary, be it the Tiber or the Neva, and end up at another, be it Syracuse or the Kolyma: riverbanks of foundation, island shores of refoundation, abysses of horror or ruin. There must surely be something of the essence in this landscape for politics to be so stubbornly represented within it. And we know that philosophy has played a signal part in this stubbornness. Its claims in respect of politics can be readily summed up as an imperative: to shield politics from the perils that are immanent to it, it has to be hauled on to dry land, set down on terra firma.

The whole political project of Platonism can be conceived as an anti-maritime polemic. The *Gorgias* insists on this: Athens has a disease that comes from its port, from the predominance of maritime enterprise governed entirely by profit and survival. Empirical politics, that is to say the fact of democracy, is identified with the maritime sovereignty of the lust for possession, which sails the seas doubly threatened by the buffeting of the waves and the brutality of the sailors. The great beast of the populace, the democratic assembly of the imperialist city, can be represented as a trireme of drunken sailors. In order to save politics it must be pulled aground among the shepherds.

From the discussion which opens Book IV of the *Laws*, we know that the distance of eighty stadia which separates the city of Clinias from its port is, in the Athenian's eyes, barely enough. Only the few encircling mountains prevent this proximity from

1

making the whole project of foundation a hopeless one. The *almuron*, the tang of brine, is always too close. The sea smells bad. This is not because of the mud, however. The sea smells of sailors, it smells of democracy. The task of philosophy is to found a different politics, a politics of conversion which turns its back on the sea.

In the first place, it is a matter of *mise-en-scène*, of shifting images around: cave and mountain instead of sea and land. Before taking us down into the famous cave, Socrates tells us a lot about triremes, incorrigible sailors and helpless pilots. Entering the cave we bid farewell to this fatal and seductive seascape. The cave is the sea transposed beneath the earth, bereft of its sparkling glamour: enclosure instead of open sea, men in chains instead of rows of oarsmen, the dullness of shadows on the wall instead of light reflected on waves. The procedure whereby the prisoner is released and offered conversion is preceded by another, by that first metaphoric act which consists in burying the sea, drying it up, stripping it of its reflections and changing their very nature. In response to these assaults we know, however, that the sea will take its revenge. For the paradox of the undertaking is that hauling politics onto the solid ground of knowledge and courage entails a return to the isles of refoundation; it means crossing the sea once more and surrendering the shepherds' resurrected city to the whims of tides and mariners.

The primary aim of this noncommittal declaration – this declaration without promises – might therefore be to indicate a few places or pathways conducive to reflection upon the figure of the boundary which has always accompanied thinking about the political; and also upon the age-old, and still current, position of philosophy at the margin of politics, always somehow linked to the idea of a retreat from that fatal brink, the idea of a change of course, of a 'conversion' which, from Greek *metanoia* to German *Kehre*, whether voluble or mute (or even mutely voluble), has always attended philosophy's thinking, or thoughtlessness, or even distractedness, vis-à-vis the political realm.

But it has also become clear that current events can give fresh meaning to this line of inquiry. Nowadays we hear countless proclamations, both scholarly and otherwise, of the end of the era in which politics wandered from littoral to littoral. Ended too, it is said, is the time when philosopher-legislators took it upon themselves to reground politics at the risk of leading it to some new abyss. Politics is apparently now at last quitting that territory, bounded by the shores of origin or blocked by the looming abyss, to which the custodianship of philosophy has hitherto confined it. Free at last, it is supposedly about to spread out through the boundless space which is that of its own suppression. The end of a subservient politics will thus also be the end of politics itself. We are said to be living through the end of political divisions, of social antagonisms and utopian projects; entering into an age of common productive effort and free circulation, of national consensus and international competition. Instead of utopian islands and millenarian dreams, the belated wisdom of our times offers more accessible earthly paradises and more imminent deadlines: Europe or the Centre, 1993 or the year 2000.

Yet, viewed from closer range, this configuration holds some surprises. Thus the same conspicuous American who noisily proclaims the end of history with our decade also tells us, more quietly, that this is the very same end proclaimed by Hegel in 1807, even if this means leaving us in doubt: Has it taken history this particularly overburdened two-centuries-long interval to get its death over with because getting rid of the last vestiges is always slow, or because of the fateful error of the interpreter, Marx, who saw in the Hegelian promise not the end of history at all, but merely the end of prehistory?

One might merely smile at the alacrity with which political administrators look forward to the time when politics will be over and they can at last get on with political business undisturbed. But it will perhaps be more interesting to take a closer look at the duplicity involved in this realization/suppression of politics, which is simultaneously a suppression/realization of philosophy. Perhaps there is something to be gained by asking questions about the new conjunction between philosophy's old claim to be steering politics away from its own fateful boundaries, and the new certainty about politics having fulfilled itself and history having ended. Is it not just when politics presumes to have freed itself from the weight of philosophical utopias that it finds itself in the very place for which it was destined by the philosophical project of doing away once and for all with the disorders of politics?

The texts which follow strive to disentangle a few analytic elements from this singular knot. They represent an attempt to get beyond today's complacent or nostalgic pronouncements about the exhaustion of egalitarian and communal (mis)adventures, about the triumph of liberal democracy or about the end of ideologies, politics and history, and identify a few paradoxes which may prompt us to reexamine not just philosophy's political role, but also the status of the peculiar activity which we call politics. The reader should be alerted to the contingent nature of these analyses and the context to which the first two texts in particular belong, namely discussions with Latin American philosophers and friends facing the hopes and difficulties of the return to democracy. In Santiago de Chile, we tried to think through a reinterpretation of how democracy is experienced beyond the theoretically and politically disastrous stereotypes of 'real' and 'formal' democracy. At a Franco-Brazilian meeting, by contrast, we considered certain ambiguities of and impasses reached by a Western democracy supposedly rejoicing over the final transcendence of class struggle. Striking students in Paris and a French presidential election eventually supplied these reflections with raw material. Though I have not hesitated to remove ambiguities or to amplify vague allusions, I hope to have preserved some feeling in what follows of direct engagement between a number of questions of interpretation within the classical philosophical tradition and a number of questions provoked by the urgencies and surprises of our own present.

The End of Politics or The Realist Utopia

1. The End of the Promise

The now ubiquitously bruited end of politics is readily described as the end of a particular period of time which is itself marked by a particular employment of time: the promise. Immediate political realities offer us a signal example of this. In 1981, we elected a new president of the Republic. At the time he made us a hundred and ten promises. Not a hundred – a hundred and ten. Excess is the essence of the promise. In 1988, we reelected him without inquiring how many of them he had kept. On the contrary, enlightened opinion praised him for the fact that this time – with a scant exception, to which I shall return – he did not make a single one. What this meant, so it was said, was that in seven years he and we had switched centuries. We were leaving behind the 'dusty philosophical and cultural corpus' of the nineteenth century, the century of the dream of the people, of promised communities and utopian islands, the century of a politics of the future which had opened up the abyss into which our own century had so nearly foundered. The new outlook of our candidate-president was supposedly that of someone who had finally seen the light, finally rounded the cape and entered the new century. For the original evil was the promise itself: the gesture which propels a *telos* of community, whose splintered parts rain back down like murderous stones. Politics was now going to renounce its long complicity with ideas of future times and other places. It would now end as a secret voyage to the isles of utopia, and henceforth view itself as the art of steering the ship and embracing the waves, in the natural, peaceful movement of growth, of that pro-duction which reconciles the Greek *phusis* with the everyday art of pushing forward one step at a time; that production which the last, mad century ruined with its murderous use of the promise.

There is one particular idea about the end of politics which goes like this: secularize politics as all other activities affecting the production and reproduction of individuals and groups have been secularized; give up the illusions attached to power, to the voluntaristic representation of the art of politics as a programme of liberation and a promise of happiness. Give up the assimilation of political *potestas* to the *imperium* of some idea, some *telos* of the group; make it more akin to the power of the secularized activities of work, exchange and pleasure. Conceive of an exercise of politics synchronous with the rhythms of the world, with the buzz of things, with the circulation of energies, information and desires: a politics exercised altogether in the present, with the future being nothing but an expansion of the present, paid for, of course, by the requisite austerities and cutbacks. Such is the new sense of time to which we are now said to be acceding. At last, they tell us, we are entering the twentieth century – several decades late.

This *is* late and no mistake. And what a peculiar configuration modern times thus takes on. Our century has apparently spent the best part of its time being no more than the future – the nightmare – of the previous one. It has only just caught up with itself, by identifying with the century to come. This two hundred-year gap is the time it has taken to get rid of the revolution, to destroy both the royal aspect of politics and the revolutionary aspect of its destruction, and so enter a homogeneous time, a temporality relieved at last of the double royalty of past and future.[1]

This time, which is no longer divided by promise, must be matched by a space freed of division. This space is 'the Centre' – meaning not one area that is central relative to others, but rather, generically, a new configuration of political space, the free development of a consensual force adequate to the free and apolitical development of production and circulation. But if it is easy to decree the beginning and ending of times, the empirical identification of this configuration poses other problems. The centre is ever elusive. The end of politics seems rather to split into two endings which do not coincide – the end of promise and the end of division – and virtually produce two politics of the 'end of politics': the party of the new time on the one hand and the party of the new consensus on the other. The French presidential election of 1988 epitomizes this. The defeated candidate had identified himself precisely with the idea of a new time. Opposite a candidate represented as the old man of promise, of the nineteenth century, he laid claim to the youth of the century to come, the dynamism of enterprise pushing new things before it. He invited us to opt simply for youth as opposed to age, to accept the now obvious fact that the exercise of power qua right (*potestas*) and the unfettered development of power qua potency (*potentia*) were one and the same. He sought to reshackle his opponent to his abandoned promises, to make him own up to the very commitments he was trying to conceal by promising nothing at all, to confess that he was ineluctably a man of promise, a man who announces what he is powerless to achieve, who casts old things far ahead instead of pushing new things before him step by step. Thus, in opposition to the man of the old promise, to the old man of promise, who neither can nor dares own up to this, there stood, in the shape of the candidate-prime minister, the man of dynamism, the one who pushes new things before him, the young man who pushes young things, the appropriate winner to carry us as conquerors into the third millennium.

This discourse argues for a potency which must, in the natural course of things, fulfil itself as power, whereas the promise tends to reduce power to impotence or madness. It is the only discourse that seems consonant with the notion of the end of promise, with the politics-beyond-ideology which now reigns absolute over all our organs of public opinion, be they popular or scholarly: a discourse that enters every corner of everyday life. Yet despite this – or perhaps because of it – it did not work when the big day came. It is as though this dominant sociological argument were meant to be sovereign every day but one – every day except the day of politics, the day of the political TV showdown when the candidates stake their all. On that day, our young, yuppy prime minister found this out: there was just no way of exacting a promise, or the betrayal of a promise, from a man who simply would not go along with it. There was no way of making him put his fatal chips in play. What needed to be done was to make him acknowledge duality, at least some conception of duality: the *Two* of promise versus potency, of word versus reality, of the men of the promise never kept versus the men of dynamism who always move forward. This discursive division dogs every argument of our time, yet there is at least one situation in which it goes unheard – either by its intended audience or by the spectators who referee the discursive duel: that situation is the clinching moment, the moment when the move from potency to power has to be made, when potency's mere display must be transformed into the proof of capacity and the right to power.

So what happened for such a 'natural' outcome to turn out so inconclusively? Very little. In face of the man who sought to capture *potestas* by means of *potentia* in order to lead us into the coming millennium, all it took was for the opponent to conjure up another boundary – not the horizon of a voyage but the brink of an abyss; for him to utter not a promise but the opposite of a promise. The very special kind of promise which I mentioned earlier: the candidate-president promised nothing but the worst – namely upheaval and civil war. Evoking this antipromise, which was assumed to have perished along with promise itself, he invoked the political to another end, another limit. And this was all he needed to negate the *Two* of promise versus potency, to affirm that he was there, in his very muteness, for one purpose only: to rally and preserve that property of Oneness which is alone capable of pulling society back from the brink of the abyss. Suddenly politics was no longer the art of advancing the energies of the world, but rather that of preventing civil war through a rational deployment of the One, of the call to unity. Apparently, multiplicity could not after all attain peace of its own accord. That such pacification might be arrived at spontaneously, through the ruin of the old dualisms, was a chimera. The relationship of the rallying *One* to the sundering *Two* was a function of an art, the art of politics, and of a virtue, the virtue of authority.

2. The Return of the Archaic

That, then, was the trick that was performed before our eyes: the promise of the worst was enough to transform the space of the end of politics, to render it archaic, to draw the *potestas* to the other side, not towards the *potentia* which was held to be its future, but towards its predecessor – the *auctoritas* of the sage. To the man who wanted to establish his potency by comparing records, there came the simple answer: we have both been equally powerless to push things before us, but we are not equal with respect to something different, with respect to the precondition of any undertaking: the sweeping aside of the threat of upheaval. In the face of this threat, *potestas* came down quite naturally on the side of the one in whom the 'spirit' of the Constitution of our Fifth Republic recognizes the supreme and cardinal virtue, *auctoritas*.

Auctoritas is the virtue which comes before the law and the exercise of power, the virtue which Livy tells us was that of the Greek Evander, son of Hermes, who resided on the banks of the Tiber, on Latin territory, before the descendants of the Trojan Aeneas, before the foundation of Rome. Evander, he tells us, compelled obedience from the shepherds *auctoritate magis quam imperio*, through the prestige vested in a person other than through the emblems and sanctions of command. Livy tells us straight away what lies behind this authority. Evander was *venerabilis miraculo litterarum*: he inspired respect through an awesome connection with the word, with what is said and what is written, with what is affirmed and interpreted by means of the word.

This then is the primary connection between *auctoritas* and the word. The *auctor* is a specialist in messages, one who is able to discern meaning in the noise of the world. Evander, the son of the messenger of the gods and of a priestess, is the obvious model here. On the riverbank, in the hubbub of a herdsmen's quarrel about stolen oxen and a murder, he is able to detect the presence of the divine, the presence of the god Hercules in the guise of the cattle thief and killer of the man responsible for the original theft. Evander recognizes the divine message and soothes the quarrel. A miracle of words.

Apparently, such miracles are still possible. As we have seen, our candidate-president refused to reply to those who wanted to pin him down on the subject of promises and make him confess to them. He said nothing. But he wrote; he wrote a letter to the French people. And discerning minds lost no time in sneering: prolix as it is, how many of its addressees are ever going to read it?

There is no limit to the naivety of such discerning minds, for whom words on paper never stand up in the face of 'reality'. Yet the answer was obvious. What did it matter how many people read the letter? What mattered was that it was signed and addressed. Not that I underestimate either the sense of democratic pedagogy, which may have inspired the author of the letter, or the civic sense and the desire for informed choice which may have created attentive readers for it. That is not the important thing, however. The important thing is that in this way it was made perfectly clear to everyone that here, in contrast to the power-hungry jogging type opposite, was a different character, a being endowed with the *miraculum litterarum* – in short, an *auctor*.

It is well known that our president likes writers. Discerning minds for whom politics is a spectacle think that in cultivating intellectuals he is playing to the gallery. But an *auctor* is something quite different from an intellectual. An *auctor* is a guarantor. He is a master of words, able to sift sense, and hence justice, from the noise of the world; to use words to quell squabbles; to unite people by apprehending meaning; to pacify by virtue of a strength that precedes the exercise of power. The *auctor* is someone able to augment (*augere*) the power of collective being, and this in a way that has very little indeed to do with the dynamism of modernity.

This then was the surprise of the moment. From the great consensus on modernization, which seemed to leave us only one choice, the choice between young and old (to which the modernity of life invariably urged the same response), an aspect of radical archaism had now emerged. The personification of youth, dynamism and production failed to get his qualities recognized as the proper credentials for taking us over the threshold of the third millennium, the millennium of a pacified society and a secularized politics. At the supposed cutting edge of modernity, at the allegedly decisive moment of the deflation of the political, what triumphed was the archaism of the old politician who succeeded in assuming the immemorial place of the *auctor* by conjuring up the gaping abyss, the brink of dread, from which he then made himself our protector. He became the guarantor of that process of pacification which was supposed to have emerged from the spontaneity of the secularized world, but which now seemed much rather to depend on an art, the archaic art of politics.

For what the old *auctor* offers is indeed the task everywhere proclaimed as that of modernity: to secularize politics, to demilitarize and diminish it, to remove everything in it which is not functionally ordained for maximizing the chances of success for the collective being, for the simple management of the social. This political task is quite precisely that of politics' self-diminution. This diminution can be described in two ways, depending on how one views the relationship between the categories of the social and the political. To diminish politics is in one sense to reduce it to its function as a pacifying procedure between individuals and collectivity by relieving it of the weight and symbols of social division. In another sense, it is to remove the symbols of political division in the interests of expansion, of society's inherent dynamism. Now this double process, the reduction of the social by the political and the reduction of the political by the social, is not something which can be carried out by the spontaneous tendencies of the century and the background hum of industry. The *One* of rational coming together relates not to the demands of the task before us, but rather to the representation of the archaic gulf which stands always as our limit. The reciprocal appeasement of the social and the political is the business of the old, an old business which politics has perhaps always had as its paradoxical essence. Politics is the art of suppressing the political.

11

It is a procedure of self-subtraction. Perhaps the end of politics is its fulfilment, the ever-young fulfilment of its oldness. And perhaps, beyond the opposition of classical and modern, philosophy has always known this duplicity of the *techne politike*, and always placed this ever-young end in close proximity to the conception of foundation.

3. Aristotle and the Centrist Utopia

To go deeply into this adjacency of the beginning and the end would entail an entire reexamination of the idea of classical political philosophy. I shall not embark on that here, but merely note one problem in passing: to endorse Leo Strauss's designation of the *Republic* and the *Politics* as works and paradigms of political philosophy is perhaps to erase the primordial tension of the relationship between philosophy and politics, the coincidence between the wish 'truly' to do political things as upheld in the *Gorgias* and the wish to put an end to politics, to hear nothing more about it. Or at least to put an end to politics in its primary spontaneous and democratic state, as the anarchic self-regulation of the many by majority decision. For Plato, the *demos* is the intolerable existence of the great beast which occupies the stage of the political community without ever becoming a single subject. The name which accurately qualifies it is *ochlos*: the common rabble or, in other words, the infinite turbulence of collections of individuals who are always at odds with themselves, living rent by passion and at the mercy of desire. On the basis of this observation an original duplicity can be defined, a relationship between philosophy and the political which is both thoroughly immanent and radically transcendent, prohibiting the existence of any such thing as 'political philosophy'.

Perhaps to a greater degree than in the radicalism of the Platonic refoundation, the complexity of this split is made plain in the more discrete tension which animates Aristotle's *Politics*. Here, the apparently simple objective of submitting the many to the law of the One is in fact split by a never entirely closed gap between two ways of conceiving the art of politics, of confronting the question of the many: politics as the organization of the human community in accordance with the *telos* of the reasonable being, and as a remedy for the sheer fact of social division. Thus the *Politics* offers us two origins for the political. There is the good origin, the one set out at the start of Book I: the distinction between the animal *phone* and the human *logos*, the peculiar power of the *logos* to project a sense of the useful (*sumpheron*) and of the harmful (*blaberon*) into the circle of the community and thereby to usher in a shared recognition of the just and the unjust. And then there is the bad origin, as set forth in Book IV, linking the logic of the principle of contradiction to the factuality of a state of things. In every city there are rich and poor. These categories constitute the elements and the parts of the city par excellence, because they designate the only principles which cannot be combined. One can always imagine that the farmers might become warriors or the artisans sit in session at the boule. But what no regime can do is make people simultaneously rich and poor. The question of politics begins in every city with the existence of the mass of the *aporoi*, those who have no means, and the small number of the *euporoi*, those who have them.

Every city has these two irreducible components, ever virtually at war, ever present and represented to each other through the names they adopt and the principles with which they identify themselves, which they make their own: liberty (*eleutheria*) for the mass of the poor, virtue (*arete*) for the small number of the rich. Thus do rich and poor constantly grasp the common thing, the middle thing, in the pincers of profit and honours, of material interests and imaginary investments.

This was a given. Ever since Solon had abolished slavery for debt in Athens, all cities had included a mass of poor people who, though unsuited to the practice of law or leadership, were nonetheless present in the city as free men, possessing the common name, the common title of the political community: freedom. Whence a second determinant of the art of politics, which is, in modern terms, the art of putting up with what cannot be reconciled, of tolerating the existence alongside the rich of the poor, who can no longer be thrown overboard and who remain attached to the centre of the city.

This primary task of politics can indeed be precisely described in modern terms as the political reduction of the social (that is to say the distribution of wealth) and the social reduction of the political (that is to say the distribution of various powers and the imaginary investments attached to them). On the one hand, to quiet the conflict of rich and poor through the distribution of rights, responsibilities and controls; on the other, to quiet the passions aroused by the occupation of the centre by virtue of spontaneous social activities.

The ideal solution, the ideal reduction of the political by the social, takes a homonym as the basis for an isomorph and dictates that the centre should be at the centre, that the political centre (the *meson*) of the city should be occupied by the middle class (*to meson*), by the class of those who are neither rich nor poor, neither *aporoi* nor *euporoi*, who need not pass, need not travel, between their social space and the political centre. Thus, the centre is no longer a pole of tension being pulled in either direction between itself and the periphery. The *archai* (or responsibilities of office) in which the *arche* (or governance of the city) is variously invested are no longer spoils which some are eager to seize or burdens which others are eager to forswear.

In this solution, as set forth in Book IV, the perfecting of politics inclines towards its self-suppression. The coincidence of the centre and the mean makes it 'altogether easy' to obey the *logos*, a *logos* which therefore appears less like the locus of a discussion than like a force which is obeyed, just as living things obey the laws of their own organisms.

Alas, this positive solution remains an ideal. Such a regime is encountered virtually nowhere. For this Aristotle offers another positive, sociological explanation: cities are too small, he says. There is no room for a middle class to develop. It is tempting to see prescience here: as opposed to the ideal of the city-democracy, Aristotle would seem to be forecasting the true future of democracy, the middle-class rule of our extended and developed modern states. But perhaps his vision was, rather, a utopia, the realist utopia; not the shimmering utopia of the distant island, of the place which does not exist, but the imperceptible utopia which consists in making two separate spaces coincide, namely

14

the social middle and the political centre. Now, we are aware that our societies produce both middle classes and tertiary sectors in abundance. But we are still searching for the centre, for the coincidence of centres. Government by the centre remains the utopia of our realist politics. For realism too is a utopia, something into which Aristotle gives us an exemplary insight. Utopia is not the elsewhere, nor the future realization of an unfulfilled dream. It is an intellectual construction which brings a place in thought into conjunction with a perceived or perceptible intuitive space. Realism is neither the lucid refusal of utopia nor the forgetting of the *telos*. It is just one utopian way of configuring the *telos*, of recovering the compass of reason within the singularity of the present. Bringing together the philosophical idea of the mean with the middle class and with the space of citizenship is still part of the attempt to carry out the Platonic project: to place the many beneath the law of the One, to institute the reign of moderation rather than that of the democratic *apeiron*. Philosophy thus puts an end to political division by mending its own division with respect to the political, by employing metaphorical resources which at once distance it utterly from empirical politics and allow it to coincide exactly with it.

The only problem, of course, is the fact that the mean never suffices to occupy the centre. And if the social fails to pacify the political, things then must be turned around and the political realm entrusted with the task of settling the problems of the social. But this the political can only do precisely by organizing its own reduction, by effacing the image of the centre and the imaginary tensions which bear upon it or radiate from it. It then falls to the art of politics to enact another coincidence between political, social and territorial space: the coincidence of distances. The art of politics is the art of putting the democratic contradiction to positive use: the *demos* is the union of a centripetal force and a centrifugal force, the living paradox of a political collectivity formed from apolitical individuals. The *demos* is forever drawing away from itself, dispersing itself in the multiplicity of ecstatic and sporadic pleasures. The art of politics must regulate the intermittency of the *demos* by imposing intervals which place its strength at a distance from its turbulence, at a distance from itself.

This is the preoccupation which characterizes Aristotle's comparison between good and bad forms of democracy in Books IV and VI of the *Politics*. A bad democracy is a democracy true to its name, where the *demos* exercises the power, where it inhabits the centre of the city, has but a few steps to take in order to sit in assembly and can lay claim to the *archai*. A good democracy, by contrast, which comes as close as possible to the ideal regime of the *politeia*, contrives to distance the *demos*. It removes the *aporoi* from the centre by means of a property qualification or by some other means. In this case 'supreme power is vested in the laws, because the state has no means [*prosodon*] of paying the citizens'.[2]

Prosodos is a remarkable word. Its primary meaning is the point where the path approaches its goal. In political parlance, this approach takes on a more precise meaning: the fact of presenting oneself to speak before the assembly. But *prosodos* also designates that surplus which makes presenting oneself, makes getting started, a possibility: the *plus* which allows one to be at the assembly at all; a surplus, therefore, with respect to work and with respect to the life which work assures. This supplement, when it is lacking, need not be an insufficiency of money. It may be simply insufficient time or leisure. A person may not have the leisure to go to the centre because the centre is distant or because the tasks and profit of the day cannot be given up in order to do so.

According to Book IV, these are the benefits of rural democracy, particularly suiting a place in which the fields are quite far from the city. Under such conditions a good democracy can exist, even a good *politeia*, because the farmers will not have the time to hold many meetings, the time to occupy the centre. They will prefer to work rather than waste their time with politics. They will have the opportunity (the *exousia*) for political activity, but they will prefer to leave the responsibilities of office to those who have the *ousia*, the wealth which makes it possible to devote one's time to it.

Here, perfection is achieved by desertion from the centre. It is necessary that the citizens be far from the centre of their sovereignty. For the regime to work, a certain quality (*poion tina*) is required. But this is not a quality possessed by the citizens, merely a property of their space. There must not be a field abutting the ramparts of the city, for the boundary must be sharply drawn, not just between the social and the political, but also between the citizens and the locus of their citizenship. There must be a hiatus, a void, at the border of the political.

Of course this no man's land is another utopia. There are always people, always a rabble on the *agora*, the populace (*ochlos*) milling around the *ecclesia*. Hence, the unbreakable rule guaranteeing the citizenship of the absent. In those democracies where 'the people are compelled to settle in the country . . . even if there is a mob (*ochlos*) on the *agora*, the assembly ought not to meet . . . when the country people cannot come'.[3] In simple terms, assembly should not be held if there are absentees: the perfect rule for an entirely self-removed democracy, the ironic inversion of the principle of the mean. The centre is assured not by presence but by absence, by virtue of a gap which serves to keep interests apart.

This realism is still utopian, however. There is no class whose mere presence or absence can pacify the sphere of the political or block all approaches to it. It therefore falls to the good politician to devise compromises that will ensure the regulation of these approaches in terms both of material arrangements and of imaginary perceptions. This entails assigning positions in such a way as to redistribute passions – to strip from what is given to some whatever makes it desirable to others. The prime example of this for Aristotle was an unpaid magistrature, which makes it possible to give everyone *exousia* while reserving the privileges of *ousia* for the few. As a result everyone will happily occupy the place appropriate to them. The poor will have no wish for magistracies and will not be jealous of those who occupy them, since they bring no remuneration. They will freely sacrifice the public passion for honour to the private passion for profit. The rich will occupy magistracies without being able to increase their wealth by doing so. They will probably even have to sacrifice a little of it. But they will pay in order to satisfy their passion, their collective point of honour: that they, the 'best', should not be ruled by the 'less good'. Thus will private and public passions be well apportioned. Moreover, the poor, the *aporoi*, being able to devote themselves entirely to work, may even become rich, become *euporoi*. One might take this to its logical extreme and say that they will thus be able to participate in their turn in the profits and losses of the *archai*. Aristotle did not do so, for he was convinced that profit is the only real passion of the masses and that they will only take an interest in politics by default. The moderns have not hesitated to take this final step, promising the poor that the very slightest advancement in wealth will propel them into the providential class of the golden mean.

Aristotle is the inventor of the essential, of modernization, of the politics of the end of the political, an end indistinguishable from the beginnings: the art of underpinning the social by means of the political and the political by means of the social. By reassigning positions and the passions that target them, by altering the perception of those positions and the emotions attending that perception, politics presides over its own erosion and creates the social realm vitally necessary to the natural realization of this goal. In the strife of being together, of *inter esse*, politics contrives intervals, the intervals that separate divergent yet coexistent *interests*. Politics thus calls forth the social dimension wherein private and public are at once harmonious and distant, as public honour and private gain are pursued with equal passion but in a mutually exclusive fashion.

One problem remains, the problem of another boundary – the boundary beyond which this perfecting of the self-diminished political realm comes closely to resemble that political negation of the political, that reabsorption of common space into the private realm of domination which is known as despotism or tyranny. Does not the best of democracies, indeed the good *politeia*, where the mass of citizens fulfil their preference for lucrative activity over the activity of citizenship, in short that good political regime which coincides with the satisfaction of citizens' apolitical needs, bring into play the very same mechanisms which serve the tyrannical annihilation of collective power: *microphronein*, the smallmindedness of individuals locked into pettiness, the idiocy of private interests; and *adunamia*, the impotence of those who have lost the resource of collective action?

Smallmindedness, mistrust and the impotence of the citizens – these are the means of tyranny, all the more liable to resemble the means of good government in that there are good tyrants, disposed of their own volition to employ those good means of social conservation described in Book VI. The model for good tyrants is Pisistratus, whose methods of government, as referred to in the *Constitution of Athens* are wellnigh indistinguishable from the rules of good rural democracy. Out of his own pocket, he advanced money to the poor for them to buy land, this with a double purpose: that they might not spend their time loitering in the city but remain dispersed in the countryside; and that with what were riches in their terms (*euporountes ton metrion*), coupled with concern for their private affairs, they might have neither the desire nor the leisure to interest themselves in common things.

The politics of dispersal. To those who may be disturbed by the similarity of the two 'ends' of politics, Aristotle offers the reassuring explanation that Pisistratus governed as a politician rather than as a tyrant and thus settles for leaving us with a paradox. Depoliticization is the oldest task of politics, the one which achieves its fulfilment at the brink of its end, its perfection on the brink of the abyss.

This political suppression of politics is also a means for philosophy to realize the closest image of political Good in the midst of the disorder of empirical politics, the disorder of democracy. This realization is enacted through a specific mediation: between the transcendence of the *telos* and the compromises of politics, Aristotle leaves room for the realist utopia of the centre, the utopia of a social realm capable of setting its own house in order, of cancelling both its own division and the divisions deriving from the passions that seek to appropriate the political centre. In the philosophical realization of the art of politics, this utopia is an evanescent moment. But the proper task of modernity has perhaps been to give substance to this evanescent middle term. Such would be the utopia of modernity – a middle term or detached fragment emancipated from the philosophical utopia: the sociological utopia; a utopia which presents its own emancipation as the emancipation of the social realm; the utopia of a rationality immanent to the social which heralds the eventual common end of philosophy and of politics.

4. Democracy Without Boundaries

It is no doubt in Tocqueville that we can best observe this advent of a sociological end to the political, in the very tension which his analysis maintains between a nostalgia for political heroism and a recognition of democracy as the peaceful self-regulation of the social. What is *Democracy in America* if not a long meditation on the contemporaneity of Aristotle? Social equality, the rule of the short view and of 'relaxed morality' as modifiers of political equality, the invasion of the *ecclesia* and the *archai* by the guttersnipe of democracy, by the mob of the *agora* – is this not the modern image of pacified democracy which comes closest to the Aristotelian notion? Tocqueville's real genius lies in his identification of a hybrid figure within modern democratic sociality, between the coming together of the centre and the coming together of what is remote from the centre. The realization of the Aristotelian project depends less on a particular class (the middle class in the centre or the citizen-farmers on the periphery) than on a particular state of the social. The pacification of the political depends upon a much deeper alteration than government by the 'golden mean', by the middle class. It depends rather on a new sociality, described as an equality of condition, which offers a truly providential solution to the regulation of the political-social relationship. What the cleverest politicians could never achieve – the creation of a self-regulated sociality automatically preventing the political from overwhelming the social or the social from overwhelming the political – is accomplished by the providential tendency for conditions to be equalized.

Equality of condition ensures the pacification of political emotions by a sort of polymerization. The elimination of passions fuelled by disjunctions and distinctions, by honours and ranks, opens up a social space where the old tensions affecting the centre are resolved by division, by the proliferation of an infinity of points of interest, of points of satisfaction of interest. The inflation of the private sphere and the multiplicity of satisfactions

associated with it, which go far beyond the mere reign of necessity or the mere desire for profit, guarantee an attachment to the
peaceful coexistence and collective discipline which make these
satisfactions simultaneously possible. A key notion in this
arrangement is relaxed morality, an equivalent to that 'facility'
(*praotes*) so highly prized by the Athenian democracy which
Plato had decried and which Aristotle had wished to safeguard,
no longer on the basis of the laxity of the populace, but rather on
the basis of a natural coincidence of the centre with the mean. By
soothing the violent passions of distance, relaxed morality effectively eases the relationship between rule and satisfaction from
the moment when, as part of the same tendency, the opposition
between rich and poor ceases to polarize political space and the
combined gains of *idion* and *koinon*, of public and private, begin
to be spread out over the entire surface of the social body; the
minimal virtue which is in the process likewise distributed to all
ensures peace better than the showy and provocative virtue of a
few. This is probably in keeping with the divine plan, even if it is
a sorry sight for those 'slightly more elevated' souls who remain
nostalgic for heroic politics.

In this way, then, the fulfilment of politics, the achievement of
measure in the midst of the unmeasured, of the democratic
apeiron, would emerge from within the *apeiron* itself in its new
mode of being. Yet there is a limit and a precondition here. The
limit is, as in Aristotle, that point where the self-distancing of the
political comes altogether to resemble despotism, the rule of a
'tutelary power' whose own facility lies in the fact that it can
exercise dominion in peace, leaving society to its state of equality, its satisfaction in the private realm and its self-regulation of
passions. The precondition is the existence of a providence. The
renunciation of the politics of honour needs the help of a providence which can discern, more clearly than those who are
nostalgic for the heroic age, what paths lead to the realization of
the Good and keep those paths well away from the roads to
despotism. The sociological utopia was in the first instance able
to emancipate itself only thanks to the secularization of providence, a secularization which was prior to the idea of progress.
Sociological providentialism was not initially a philosophy of

21

progress, but a bulwark against decadence, a way of reinterpreting what was originally apprehended as decadence.

The so-called postmodern age is a time when this reinterpretation of 'decadence' imagines itself capable of emancipation from every reference to providence. Nowadays, we are told, the polarization of rich and poor has been sufficiently erased to carry away in its wake the fevers that attend political honour and heroic democracy. Democracy has passed the age of its archaic fixations, which used to transform even the enfeebled difference between rich and poor into a fatal point of honour. It is now all the more secure for having been perfectly depoliticized, for being no longer perceived as the object of a choice but lived as an ambient milieu, as the natural habitat of postmodern individualism, no longer imposing struggles and sacrifices in sharp contradiction with the pleasures of the egalitarian age.

The question of space is thus resolved by means of a void: the absence of any visible gap, any brink, any precipice. *The Era of the Void* is the title of a book by Gilles Lipovetsky that caused something of a stir.[4] The author rejects pessimistic analyses of the contradiction between contemporary hedonism on the one hand and the economic demand for effort and the political demand for equality on the other. Instead, he assures us of an ever more perfect consonance between democratic pluralism and the triumph of a 'process of personalization', promoting and generalizing a type of individual who lives in a permanent universe of freedom, of choice and of relaxed and lighthearted attitudes to choice itself. 'As narcissism grows', writes Lipovetsky,

> democratic legitimacy wins out, even if it does so in the 'cool' mode. The democratic regimes with their party pluralism, their elections and their freedom of information are ever more clearly akin to the personalized society of self-service, psychological testing and permutable freedom.

Such scholarly analyses are echoed in the banal themes of the pluralist society, where commercial competition, sexual permissiveness, world music and cheap charter flights to the Antipodes quite naturally create individuals smitten with equality and tolerant of difference. A world where everyone needs everyone else, where everything is permitted so long as it is on offer as individual pleasure and where everything is jumbled together is proposed to us as a world of self-pacified multiplicity. Reason is supposed to flower here in its least vulnerable form: not as discipline forever threatened by transgression and delegitimation, but as a rationality produced by development itself, as a consensual deregulation of the passions. Pluralism thus is today's name for the point of concord, of utopian harmony, between the intoxication of private pleasures, the morality of equality in solidarity, and sensible Republican politics.

5. The End Disrupted

Thus did we row towards the happy shores of the free exchange of goods, bodies and candidates. But in this world all happiness comes to an end, even the happiness of the end itself. Realist utopias are, like other kinds, subject to the shock of the real. The electoral conjuncture which gave us the young entrepreneur disarmed before the old *auctor* had yet other means of teaching us that the triumph of youth currently identified with the pacification of politics is not very suitable for this purpose. The four million votes cast for the candidate of 'France for the French' amounted to a brutal awakening: in the face of the supposed collapse of the political sphere, with the party of the rich and the party of the poor both calling for modernization and nothing else, with the only choice – given the nearly identical nature of the enterprise as envisaged by either side – being to opt for the better-tailored public-relations image; in the face of all this, what emerged, stunningly, was not consensus but exclusion, not reason become the social rationality of the coexistence of satisfactions, but pure hatred of the Other, a coming together in order to exclude. Where politics was supposed to be catching up with the times, dropping dogmas and taboos, what appeared centre-stage was not what was expected: not the triumph of a modernity without prejudices, but the return of the supremely archaic, of that which precedes all judgement – hatred.

The party of the 'young' and 'dynamic' finally got around to understanding this. Discussing records and promises, candidates' ages and programmes was not the real issue. It is not very clever to claim victory in a debate with the man who occupies the place of the father by showing him that he is old. That goes without saying. You cannot expect to defeat the father by debating with him. The tack to follow in such cases is not the youthful call to enterprise but the age-old call to hatred. So, plastered around the streets, we saw the black silhouette of the father as of a man to be shot down. This was definitely more to the point. Against the man who drapes himself in the *miraculum litterarum*, the best answer is the baying of the wolf pack. Against the *archaion*, the *archaioteron*, the even more archaic. Against the father figure of the politician, the figure of the father to be killed.

As a peaceful end to the political, this suspiciously resembles its murderous prehistory, casting serious doubt on the idea that the society of the free exchange of goods, bodies and simulacra is one and the same thing as the society of consensual pluralism. Of course such doubt is not new – not since *Civilization and Its Discontents*. But, by a curious coincidence, the pessimistic prediction which contested the Marxist promise sixty years ago keeps getting obscured by assurances of peace predicated upon the decline of that promise. And we need the brutal fact of events to remind us: relaxed attitudes are perhaps not exactly the most characteristic feature of the economy of pleasure. Rather than tolerance, what it meets with is the irregulability of a primal horror, the irregulability of hatred and dread, the pure rejection of the other.

A pure rejection which it is too convenient to put down to frustration, as the incorrigibly rose-coloured realists would have us do. For them, hatred originates in disputes over property or position, when the other possesses something one lacks. For example, you hate Arabs because you are unemployed and they have jobs. Yet again, the seductiveness of coincidences, wretched as they might be: in this hypothesis you hate because you are deprived, you exclude because you are excluded. This happens, of course. But everyday experience still teaches us that the pleasures of exclusion scarcely diminish with the comfort and stability of one's own position. Putting hatred down to lack is giving oneself licence to see the issue as merely one of back-wardness in modernity, as a relic of the obsolete war between rich and poor. There are, it is said, those left behind by expansion. They are still in the last century because we have not had enough time yet for everyone to benefit from the fruits of growth.

Time then, in a headlong flight, becomes the substance of the last utopia. All we need is to have no lack of it, all we need is not to be missing from it, and politics will attain its appointed end. We would have it that the age of promises and progress is over. But what has expired is not so much a progressivist faith in the powers of time as the link which that faith once maintained with the idea of a yardstick, a *telos* which served simultaneously to take the measure of the state of politics and give a finality to its forward motion. Now, with neither yardstick nor end, it is faith in the pure form of time which must serve as the last utopia, the one which survives the disappointment occasioned each time utopia is spatialized. This utopia conflates two characterizations of time. On the one hand, time as the form of the infinite, of the *apeiron* to which all problems of measure and measurelessness can be referred as to their natural place; on the other, time as the principle of growth opposing the only remaining identifiable evil: delay, which is the source of lack. What then becomes even more sovereign than the idea of the technical domination of the world is the idea of time as pure self-expansion. The new millenarianism tells us that in 1993 or 2000 we shall enter into continuous, homogeneous time, a time without events, for which no event can have the function of a yardstick. In contrast to our recent obituary bicentennials, these dates herald the end of that time when dates interrupted time, when events had ensuing effects. What is heralded in its stead is a time in which every political commandment will embrace the natural form of 'Forward! March!'. Time, then, as the panacea not just for the sorrows of the heart but for all political evils. All we need is time, give us time, clamour all our governments. Of course every government wants to increase its life span. But there is more in this plea: the transfer to time of all utopian powers. Education policies exemplify this with the equation: education = job training. This equation implies much more than its obvious meaning – giving the young at school qualifications which match the jobs on the market – because it posits a utopian equivalence between the biological time of the child's maturing into adulthood and the temporality of the expanding market.[5] In the final phase of the secularization of providence, faith in nature, in the natural productivity of time, becomes synonymous with faith in miracles.

To the provocation of a certain return of the archaic, of a certain reversal of the 'end', the realist utopia responds with a headlong flight which is also a theory of headlong flight. If we do not want to let ourselves be dragged into the recklessness of this flight, we shall have to consider the question against the grain, to take seriously this reversion to the archaic, these new outbursts of hatred for the Other and these repetitions of the ancestral gesture of appeasement. Do these not testify to a peculiar drift concerning the collapse of the dualistic principle, of the way in which conflict is represented? Where the social principle of division, the war between rich and poor, is pronounced dead and buried, we see the rise of the passion for the excluding One. Politics thus finds itself facing an even more radical split, born neither of differences in wealth nor of the struggle for office, but rather of a particular passion for unity, a passion fed by the rallying power of hatred.

6. The Philosopher and the Politician

This blind spot of the realists may also be the blind spot of a philosophy which is often, when it comes to politics, more 'realist' than is generally acknowledged. Let us return to the twofold origin, the twofold determination of the political in Aristotle: a nature which makes man an eminently political being, and the contingent fact of the division between rich and poor. The gulf between these two theses prompts the question whether the whole issue can indeed be summed up simply by evoking, first, the natural sociability of those who share the *logos* and, second, the primary opposition which is necessarily the stance of those who are what the others are not, who do not have what the others have. This 'between-the-two' problem may well be connected to a strange figure who makes a furtive appearance in Book I of the *Politics*: the apolitical individual, a being with neither hearth nor home who is either 'above humanity' or else abject (*phaulos*, an adjective so pejorative as to have no comparative). This being, Aristotle tells us, this cityless being, is a lover of war in that he is an *azux*, a non-cooperator, an 'isolated piece at draughts'.[6]

This proposition would seem strange even if we were better acquainted with the play and terminology of the game referred to.[7] Yet there is nothing isolated about the proposition itself, which is firmly embedded in Aristotle's argument: it comes directly after the assertion of something considered manifest (*phaneron*), namely that man is by nature a political animal; and it is followed by another 'obvious fact' (*delon*), one which seems, if not to be directly inferable from it, then at least to be buttressed by it: the fact, once again, that man is a political animal – distinctly more political, at any rate, than bees or other gregarious animals.

Between these two obvious facts, then, comes this nonetheless odd proposition: the desire for war is a property of the isolated man. On whom then would he make war? Unless 'state of war' simply means 'state of solitude'. Draughts will scarcely suffice to enlighten us; the game seems much rather to be there to close the question. This may be customary. In Plato, a reference to gaming had already been used to cut argument dead; in both the *Republic* and the *Politics* the reference serves to suggest that a mass out of which so few elite players emerge is even more unfit to furnish the rulers of the city. Here, it closes the door on a different question: the question of a being-together which could be a conductor of hate, a contributor to war. Only two forms of combat are in prospect here. There is the war brought by the asocial individual, by he who is more or less than a man. This unthinkable, inexplicable war remains an academic hypothesis, since it assumes a nature other than human nature. And then there is the combat between groups on the basis of the distribution of property and prerogatives, which politics can pacify by redistributing the cards or by changing the perception of the game.

A state of solitude, then, or a collective struggle for what the

27

other group possesses. The excluded middle here, the 'between-the-two' which is not conceptualized, is the socialization of hatred, the community formed not to seize the property of another community, but simply for the sake of and on the basis of hatred. This is the *archaioteron* with which the *arche* must deal, most ancient of all, yet still young as the millennium of the obsolete class struggle hoves in sight: the blind spot at the boundary of the political which is also the blind spot of a philosophy that conceives of war as division and hatred as envy, whereas in fact hatred is a rallying force in its own right and rallies for no reason but the precise fact that for each individual it is simply there, prior to any cause or reason being imagined and having no conceivable purpose for nature that makes signs (those *semeia* or signs of nature which are so much in evidence when Aristotle demonstrates the political nature of the human animal). Spinoza at any rate must have encountered this hatred in the murderous frenzy of the *ultimi barbarorum* – the citizens of that nation of merchant capital which pioneered our boundless modernity. Yet measuring the modernity of this barbarism would surely have compelled him to ruin his philosophical edifice, to acknowledge a rift in the empire of nature: not the risible pretension of an empire governed by human will, but, on the contrary, the irreducible region of a distress resistant to that knowledge which changes sadness into joy.

This is an area that philosophy has trouble approaching, whether its relationship to the ignorant mass be patient (Spinoza) or impatient (Plato): that point where the order of the pack becomes clearly distinct from the disorder of popular movements; that junction of the one and the many which is neither the union of the discordant many nor the resolution of the contradiction, but the place where the terrors of the One meet the terrors of the many, where the dread of the disarmed subject, of the child-subject evoked by Jean-François Lyotard,[8] becomes the face of a mobilizing hatred, where the cure for separation turns into radical evil. Is this not the point which philosophy avoids even at its most radically self-accusatory, even when it deems its betrayal of its own task the very foundation of the totalitarian catastrophe? Is not the peculiarity of the Heideggerian approach to politics that it swallows up the question of a rallying hatred in the supposedly more radical abyss of philosophy's catastrophe and self-punishment? In the terror of the century, philosophy refuses to acknowledge any principle but its own original error: the old but ever young betrayal called metaphysics, which abandons the task of illuminating what is in the imperilled light of being and instead sets up an all-powerful subject presiding over a world of objects placed at its disposal; this principle of the omnipotence of the subject and of the devastation of the world fulfils itself in the reign of technology, while the political terror it exerts appears as just one of its achievements (the corpses in the gas chamber, certainly, but also the land laid waste by agribusiness, and so forth).

We know how drastically this precipice principle resolves the issue of the approach to politics. By positing a single essence of domination as the unified principle of our time, it prohibits the giving of meaning to the *Two* of politics in whatever form (Nazism and social democracy, bourgeoisie and proletariat, democracy and totalitarianism). America and Russia necessarily exemplify the working of this same principle: the same frenzy of unrestrained technology, the same normalization of the rootless individual. And what disappears in this account is the singularity of rallying-to-exclude, along with its most radical, exterminatory, expression. The shared brink of the abyss leaves room for only two possibilities: either a voluntaristic *metanoia* turning its back to the sea and opposing the common drift of the rows of American and Soviet oarsmen so as to bring a saved people back to dry land – back to earth, to the values of the earth (with all the homonymic resonances this suggests); or else a reversal of the century, the flash of light in the depths of suffering, the wait for which is led by thought, distancing itself, interminably philosophizing philosophy away, mimicking the self-reduction of the political in an extraordinary passion for self-mortification.

Strangely, it is the same self-reductive figure which serves those who confront the question of how the philosopher of the century – one who spent his life warning his time of the horror for which it was heading – could have become complicitous with the most extreme form of this horror. The answer given is always based on locating the point where thought has forgotten to set a space between itself and its metaphysical double – the point where the fields still come right up to the city ramparts. The aim is to identify the concept that has not yet been deconstructed, the concept whose survival is what makes possible such support for the abhorrent. Apparently there are always surplus words, words which, in becoming literal, plunge the thinker into the unconceptualized abyss. There are always more of these words to be purged, and demonstrably no would-be purger ever completely finishes the job.

Perhaps this approach is more attached than it likes to think to the doxies of a century that fiercely systematizes its mistrust of words (which, it is said, are never innocent) precisely because this mistrust has so regularly proved vain. There is nothing for it: there will always be surplus words, just as there are always fields abutting the ramparts or a mob pressing around the *ecclesia*. The many, in whatever form they appear, will continue to hold sway. No matter how many words are taken away, one can never silence the cries that stir up the crowd. Hence, the somewhat hollow pathos of philosophy's sacrificing itself to expiate its sins, consuming itself in a flame supposed at once to shed light on and constitute reparation for the horrors of the century. All this spectacular reparation really does is leave it to the practitioners of politics to deal concretely with hatred. This then is the task entrusted to the king-guarantor of democracy: to define a coming together so that dispersal is reduced without unleashing the kind of unification that is based on hate; and to define it in its necessary relationship to an 'at least Two' representing neither the simple factuality of the division of social forces, nor the romance of enlightening debate, but rather the site of a common *catharsis* of the passions of the one and of the many, the point of minimum constriction of what cannot live peacefully either under the regime of the one or under the regime of dispersal.

Should this constriction, this jostling between the One and the Two for the government of the many, be perceived as a simple matter of the sensible view, forever devoid of any *logos*? Or even worse, a matter of *empeiria* – of the sort of jiggery-pokery with

30

which Socrates taxes the rhetoric of the emulators of Gorgias, or in the sense in which we still speak of electoral jiggery-pokery? Should we not rather take a different route and return to that initial point, that inaugural moment when philosophy, in order to conjure away the disorder of the *ochlos* and the evil of division, invented for itself and for the politics to come the politics of the end of politics? At this initial point, philosophy got the root evil wrong, as it were, misapprehending the true figure of the *ochlos*, which is not the disordered turbulence of the many but the hate-driven rallying around the passion of the excluding One. Is it not this initial misjudgement which is revisiting us when in place of the clamour of a now obsolete division we once again hear the howling of the pack? Perhaps we need to reconsider the factuality of democratic division, and ponder the fact that the political war between the parties and the social war between rich and poor, upon whose passing we have been congratulating ourselves, had, in themselves and in their conflictual interrelationship, an ill-appreciated power to remedy the evil at the root. It is as though the war between rich and poor had also in some sense pacified an older war. As though the double division of the political and the social did after all have a regulating function in relation to the more radical schism provoked by that particular kind of passion for unity whose rediscovery of archaic gestures and charismas of pacification are the corollary of the erasure of division itself.

7. Democracy and Ochlocracy: From Plato to Post-Socialism

If we are to think through the present meaning of the 'end of politics' we shall have to reconsider the relationship posited by Greek thought between the *demos* and the *ochlos*, between the power of the people and the turbulent unification of individual turbulences. Modern ideas of democracy have generally confirmed this initial model, directly or indirectly, by identifying democracy either with the self-regulation, in the final instance, of dispersed focuses of use and profit, or with the power of the law which institutes collective sovereignty by submitting the particular to the universal. But if the *ochlos* from the outset is not the disordered sum of appetites but the passion of the excluding One – the frightening rallying of frightened men – the relation must be conceived otherwise. The *demos* might well be nothing but the movement whereby the multitude tears itself away from the weighty destiny which seeks to drag it into the corporeal form of the *ochlos*, into the safety of incorporation into the image of the whole. Democracy is neither the consensual self-regulation of the plural passions of the multitude of individuals nor the reign of a collectivity unified by law under the shadow of Declarations of Rights. Democracy exists in a society to the degree that the *demos* exists as the power to divide the *ochlos*. This power of division is enacted through a contingent historical system of events, discourses and practices whereby any multitude affirms and manifests itself as such, simultaneously refusing both its incorporation into the One of a collectivity that assigns ranks and identities and the pure abandonment of individual focuses of possession and terror.[9] Democracy does not exist simply because the law declares individuals equal and the collectivity master of itself. It still requires the force of the *demos* which is neither a sum of social partners nor a gathering together of differences, but quite the opposite – the power to undo all partnerships, gatherings and ordinations. The genius of Plato clearly grasped that this force of the anonymous many as such amounted to a revolt of the cardinal against the ordinal. For him, of course, this revolt could only be that of the mass, the disordered sum of disordered focuses of appetite. But the claim of modern democracy turns this thesis on its head. It stands against all ordination – all 'geometric' equality – by positing the *demos* as the autonomous power to separate from the *ochlos*, that is to say from the animal rule of politics in either its conjoined or its disjoined forms: the One of collectivity, the distribution of social ranks or the helotism of individuals. This specific power of the *demos*, which exceeds all the dispositions of legislators, is in its simplest form the rallying-dividing power of the primal many, the power of the *Two* of division. The Two of division is the path followed by a *One* which is no longer that of collective incorporation but rather that of the equality of any One to any other One.

The essence of equality is in fact not so much to unify as to declassify, to undo the supposed naturalness of orders and replace it with the controversial figures of division. Equality is the power of inconsistent, disintegrative and ever-replayed division which tears politics away from the various figures of animality: the great collective body, the zoology of orders justified in terms of cycles of nature and function, the hate-driven rallying of the pack. The inconsistent division of the egalitarian argument deploys its humanizing power through specific historical forms. In the modern democratic age, declassifying division has taken on a privileged form whose name has fallen totally out of favour, yet if we are to know where we are we must look at this form face-on. The name given to this privileged form was class struggle.

Against the old feudal dream of the great collective body divided into orders and its new scholarly or vulgar variants, against the new 'liberal' dream of the weights and counterweights of a pluralist society guided by its elites, class struggle proclaimed and placed at the heart of the democratic conflict the humanizing power of division. In the first place, being a member of the militant class means only this: no longer being a member of a lower order. To name the opposition between bourgeois and proletarians is to institute a single locus of polemical division as a means of asserting the unacceptability of all unequal distribution, all fixing of social ranks on the model of animal species. Consequently, the declaration of class struggle initially took two distinct forms, both equally apt to derail those zoologists inclined to search for its secret in the lower depths of working-class ways of life or in the difference between archaic and modern, or skilled and unskilled, working-class strata. The first is to be found in the 'naivety' of those working-class pamphlets which take as their battle standard the statement that *there are no* classes, the second in the sophistication of the theoretician who proclaims the proletariat as a *non-class* of society, as the dissolution of all classes. The difficult encounter between Marx and proletarian socialists is played out on the razor's edge of this paradoxical question: how are we to conceive of the agent of this action of declassification? How to name this agent if not still by the class name? This name will then mean two contradictory things. On the one hand, it will designate the dissolution of classes actually taking place – which is to say also the dissolution of the working class by itself, the work on itself which tears it away both from the animality of corporatism and from the animality of the pack. But at the same time it will fix the class which effects the declassification in its own substantivity, thereby resuscitating the fantasy of a good distribution of social functions or, in other words, in the final analysis, introducing a new form of the fantasy of the well-ordered One.

All the conflicts in the 'working-class movement' have had at heart the naming of this non-class class, of this insubstantial substantiality. Marx thought he had given this contradiction adequate form in the figure of that party which united proletarians by dividing the class whose party it was. That this figure should have turned out historically to be the most fearsome of exemplars of the One that subjugates, indeed the exemplar most apt to substantiate all the others, because it cumulated the powers of imaginary incorporation, of feudal stratification and of the isolation of terrified individuals, can hardly be said to have eliminated the problem. By forgetting Marx, however long the list of good reasons for doing so, we sorely risk simultaneously forgetting the other side of the contradiction: the movement which has nourished the democracies of the declassifying, demassifying power of the class struggle. Indeed, no matter how vigorously democracy has applied itself to reducing the class struggle to something incongruous in a free, equal and fraternal order, and no matter how vigorously the class struggle for its part has sought to denounce democracy as a front for domination, the fact remains that each has found itself bound to the other, bartering the powers of the One, which denies exclusion for the powers of the Two, which exposes that exclusion and reopens the conflict; each has shared its culture with the other, and each has done far more to form and civilize the other than all the 'permissiveness', all the self-service and all the free trade in bodies and goods put together. To forget Marx is thus to forget this simple question: beyond class struggle, what will play the part of that division which separates *demos* from *ochlos*? Just as pure progressivism (pure faith in the powers of time) succeeds the

34

progressivism of a society advancing boldly towards the realization of its *telos*, what succeeds forgotten Marxism is a
bastardized Hegelianism: the peaceful realization of reason by a
government of the wise against the backdrop of consensual, con-
sumerist mediocracy. Ochlocracy fulfilled takes the form of that
government of wise men which is alone fit to administer the
unharmonious harmony of proliferating focuses of satisfaction.
Postdemocracy is perhaps the precise coincidence of ochlocracy
with its supposed opposite, *epistemocracy*: government by the
most intelligent, emerging quite naturally from the regime of the
education system to effect the precisely calculated administration
of the infinity of great and small focuses of satisfaction. As we
know, however, the limitation of administrators of satisfaction is
how hard they find it to manage two or three related emotions
which are less easily quantifiable and indexible: frustration, fear
and hate. This is where an additional intervention is called for,
that of the good king, the democratic king, skilled at executing
two gestures in one – at exemplifying the One just sufficiently to
pacify the passions of the pack and thereby preserve the *demos* as
an abode of duality. The king ever ready, also, to cry wolf as a
way of bringing the wolf to the door – of forcing things to the
brink of the abyss so that his peacemaking becomes essential.

Are we under a monarchy? asks a would-be provocative voice
from time to time. What calls forth the singular figure of the
democratic king leading us with repetitive archaic gestures
towards a boundless postmodernity is actually a newer figure,
that of the conflict between democracy and ochlocracy. Were
they to misjudge the scope of this conflict, our managers of the
end of politics would no doubt have to set off in search of other
returns of the archaic. But the question facing the politicians
also impinges on philosophy, whose original position placed it
face to face with a democracy which constituted absolute otherness for it, because it enshrined the scandal of the factuality of
the many making the law. Perhaps the caricature of itself that is
now a commonplace of enlightened politics and serious journal-
ism will compel philosophy more resolutely to explore the path
of another idea of factuality, namely the path of the wisdom of
the many – a path, moreover, which the tireless genius of

Aristotle long ago traced, along with the path of the centrist utopia, in more than one passage of the *Politics*. For it would indeed be the ultimate scandal for philosophy, the highest price it could pay for its Platonic arrogance in face of the empiricists, if it were obliged to leave to the sole judgement of political jiggery-pokery, not just the conduct of the people's business, but what is perhaps philosophy's own most intimate business: how to deal with fear and hate.

Notes

1   The end of this interval has sometimes been described as 'the end of the French exception', but France certainly has no monopoly on violent beginnings for rational democracy, even if some people have come to the conclusion in all sincerity that the English parliamentary regime was the product of a harmonious union between royal wisdom and free industrial expansion, or that American democracy arose solely from the combination of the spirit of enterprise and Puritan morality. The true meaning of this 'end of the exception' was revealed by the renditions of 'La Marseillaise' with which Eastern Europe responded to our pompous and revanchist interment of the Bicentennial, for they resituated it within that movement which began in the England of the Stewarts and which has not yet run its course.

2   Aristotle, *Politics*, IV, 1292b, 37–8.

3   Ibid., VI, 1319a, 36–8.

4   Gilles Lipovetsky, *L'ère du vide, Essais sur l'individualisme contemporain*, Paris 1983.

5   What is more, this utopia impinges on the means suggested for actualizing the equation. In the bulky educational reform plans generated by any minister worth his salt, one particular kind of proposal absolutely always turns up: I am referring to proposals affecting the organization of time. Proposals for shorter school days or longer school years, for cutting lessons by five minutes or rescheduling terms and vacations. Of course, all such measures are always backed up by appeals to psychological and pedagogical authorities, and they have the added charm of being the least costly. But what is more significant about their persistent presence is the eloquent testimony it bears to a faith in the magical powers of time – powers such that any manipulation of time at all, even a blind one, guarantees some miraculous result or other.

6   Aristotle, *Politics*, I, 1253a, 5–6.

7   Draughts or backgammon offer only approximate equivalents to the *pettoi* or pebbles which came into several ancient Greek games. The precise nature of the game evoked here has been debated notably by Becq de Fouquières (*Les jeux des anciens*, Paris 1869) and H. Jackson (*Journal of Philology*, vol. 7, 1877). On the basis of the commentaries, despite their divergences and uncertainties, it seems we may assume that the *azux* piece was a fixed piece able to check any other piece approaching it in an adjacent

space, and not an isolated piece liable to be encircled in the course of the play (for there is a difference in kind between pieces). The exact text and syntax of this entire passage has been much discussed.

8   See 'Le survivant', in Hannah Arendt, *Ontologie et politique*, Paris 1989.

9   The problems of imaginary incorporation and democratic division are central to Claude Lefort's work. The notion of any given multitude has received systematic philosophical treatment in Alan Badiou, *L'être et l'évènement*. Despite this necessary reference to two very different intellectual projects, responsibility for the ideas set forth here, using a similar terminology, is solely the author's.

2

The Uses of Democracy

Modern thinking on democracy has often represented it as distanced from itself, separated from its truth. Those who congratulate themselves most loudly on enjoying its benefits willingly reduce it to a consensus that inegalitarian order is best suited to supplying the disadvantaged with their minimum share of power and well-being. Those, on the other hand, who emphasize democracy's call for equality are quick to respond, stressing the stubborn reality of an inequality which gives it the lie. With regard to representative democracy and the theories which maintain it, the socialist tradition has long denounced the implied fiction of an ideal community, a fiction serving merely as a mask for the reality of selfishness and class exploitation. And the collapse of the socialist model has certainly not dispelled the suspicion that the democracy to which we in the West pay homage is but a shadow of the real thing. Real democracy would presuppose that the *demos* be constituted as a subject present to itself across the whole surface of the social body. The empirical figure of democratic man seems to contradict the full idea of the democratic community.

This vision is expressed, for example, in C.B. Macpherson's book *The Life and Times of Liberal Democracy*, where liberal democracy appears as the somewhat unnatural conjunction of democracy's communal essence and the individual reckoning of profits and costs in the liberal universe of the interest-adjusting invisible hand.[1] If left to themselves, democracy and individualism would go in opposite directions. And in the current atmosphere of disillusionment we would seem to have the choice between only two positions: either to recollectivize the idea of democracy, while accepting liberal democracy as an irreversible fact (whence the search for an injection of more soul, as epitomized by the idea of participation); or else to frankly accept that what we call democracy is nothing but liberalism, that all the dreams of happy polities have never been anything but dreams, the self-deceit of a society of big and small capitalists who are finally complicit in the advent of the reign of the possessive individual.

I wonder whether these dilemmas do not imply certain false assumptions about the nature of democracy. At the heart of these false assumptions is a strange notion about the original democracy, about ancient democracy: it is as though this had been a system founded on the continuous presence of the people-as-subjects, and as though this system had been contested and ruined from within by the coming of capitalist individualism and by the emergence of a subject made docile, even in its proletarian form, by that individualism. This view embodies revolutionary and romantic nostalgias for a beautiful totality of citizenship, which serve paradoxically to buttress liberalism's conviction of having only just invented the individual, and it offers an image of Greek democracy which ignores the very features which that democracy ascribed to itself.

1. The Reign of the Many

Let us recall for a moment a founding text of democracy's reflections on itself: the funeral oration delivered by Pericles in Book II of Thucydides' *History of the Peloponnesian War*. This speech immediately proposes a concept of freedom which treats it as the unity of two ideas: a particular idea of the *public* and a particular idea of the *private*. In the words that Thucydides puts in his mouth, Pericles says something like this: in public we conduct the affairs of the city; as for the private, as for the affairs of the individual, we leave those to be handled as each person thinks fit.

The concept of freedom unifies the private and the public, then, but it unifies them in their very separateness. Essentially, Pericles says that our political regime is not one of mobilization. We do not prepare for war after the fashion of the Spartans. Our military preparation resembles our life itself, a life without constraints and without secrets. The democratic political subject has a shared domain in the very separateness of a way of life characterized by two great features: the absence of constraints and the absence of suspicion. Suspicion, in Thucydides' Greek, is called *hypopsia*: looking underneath. What characterizes democracy for Thucydides is the rejection of this looking underneath – something which the social theorists of the modern age elevate, by contrast, to the rank of a theoretical virtue, an appropriate means of apprehending, beneath the appearance of commonality, a truth which belies it.

Nothing, of course, compels us to take Pericles, or Thucydides, at his word, to identify Athenian democracy with its discourse on itself in this or that particular circumstance. In *L'Invention d'Athènes*, Nicole Loraux reminds us that this speech of Pericles was indeed a speech intended to mobilize. And we know, for example, that Athenian practices of denunciation, or the use of *antidosis*, involved keeping a fairly close eye on one's neighbours' actions, not to mention a close check on their property. Still, there is at least one idea here which is so consistent that adversaries and devotees of democracy alike can subscribe to it: the idea that from the outset democracy connects a particular practice of political community with a style of life characterized by the sporadic. The man of the democratic city is not a permanent soldier of democracy. It is this sporadic character which one adversary of democracy, Plato, mocked in Book VIII of the *Republic*, describing equality as conceived by the democratic man as the incapacity to prioritize, to choose between the necessary and the superfluous, the equal and the unequal. The democratic man, for Plato, wants equality in everything, even in the unequal; not recognizing the difference between the necessary and the superfluous, he considers everything, including democracy, on the basis of desire, change or fashion. On one day, Plato tells us, he will intoxicate himself with the sound of his flute, then on the next he will fast; one day he will take exercise, the next he will lie around; one day he will engage in politics, the next in philosophy; for a time he will pursue the arts of war, then forsake war for business and so forth.

We could easily translate this portrait into modern terms: Plato's democratic man, moving from politics to dieting or from the gym to philosophy, bears a fair resemblance to what is described to us as the postmodern individual. But whereas the schizophrenic individual of consumer society is readily identified with the ruination or degeneration of democracy, Plato anticipates himself as a caricature of democracy's perfect incarnation. For Plato, democracy is in its essence a system of variety, and this applies equally well to what is on offer politically: democracy, he says, is not a constitution, but a bazaar filled with all possible constitutions, where anyone can choose to perceive whichever variety they please.

Thus, as seen by an opponent, democracy is the regime of multiple accommodations. This idea of the regime which everyone can see differently recurs in Aristotle, but Aristotle conceives this strength of multiple accommodation not as a sign of inferiority but as a political virtue. This virtue is certainly not that of democracy for Aristotle, however. For him, as for Plato, democracy is only the least bad of bad regimes; it is a regime off course as compared with the correct regime, with the *politeia* – in other words, with the Republic. But on the other hand, the good regime is characterized precisely by the fact that it is always a mixture of constitutions, a constitutional marketplace. A regime without mixture, a regime which wants all its laws and institutions to resemble its basic principle, condemns itself to civil war and ruin because of the very unilateralism of this principle. In order to approach perfection, each regime must therefore correct itself, striving to welcome opposing principles, to make itself unlike itself. There is never such a thing as a good regime, in fact, only regimes off course engaged in the perpetual work of self-correction – one might almost say of self-dissimulation. Thus to Plato's mockery of the marketplace of regimes might well be opposed the passage in Book IV of the *Politics* where Aristotle argues that there should appear to be elements of both types of regime (oligarchy and democracy) and yet at the same time of neither, a good polity being one in which the oligarch sees oligarchy and the democrat democracy.[2]

It is worth pausing to consider the function of artifice here, for it embodies all the complexity of Aristotle's conception of politics. Simultaneously discrediting the realist utopia of coincidence and the purely manipulative conception of politics, it opens onto an idea of politics not as illusion or machination but as the art of life in common. In Aristotle, artifice actualizes that principle of life in common which goes by the name of friendship, thwarting the unilateralism characteristic of each of the constitutive elements of politics. It is a way of playing the other's game, of catching him out at his own game, and it cannot be reduced to some 'cunning of reason'. For Aristotle, this art remains the science of the ruler, but perhaps a portion of what has been called 'democratic invention' consists in the ability with which the non-rulers enable themselves to play the game.

From this rapid survey of certain founding statements of democracy and the Republic, let me draw two observations:

1. Democracy – the power of the *demos* – is not synonymous with some principle of unity and ubiquity. The power of the *demos* is just as much that of a style of life which gives the private and the public their due.

2. The art or artifice of life in common, the way in which a regime must make itself unlike itself, may still have something to do with the thinking and practice of politics under modern democracy. Perhaps there is a connection to be found between the art of dissemblance as theorized by Aristotle and the principle of division which Claude Lefort sees as the essence of modern democracy, as the site of a disembodied power, splintered between diverse agencies of legitimacy, in particular the agencies of the law and of knowledge.

We know that this regime of division has usually been conceived of as something negative, as the manifestation of a sundering, a non-truth, of democracy. Critical social thought has been strangely contaminated by a problematic born of theocratic counterrevolutionary thought, which depicts the emergence of democracy as a loss of unity, a sundering of the social bond. I shall not dwell on all the aspects of this fantasy of a totality lost and yet to be restored which the counterrevolution has so generously bequeathed to socialism and social science. My problem is not the question of whether the principle of totalitarianism is or is not to be located here. It is rather to see how this idea of division as non-truth – as lie or illusion – has been transposed into social science and into the forms of social critique and political perception that have been affected by it. For it was indeed this idea that gave social science its original character as a science of suspicion which conceives the heterogeneity of democratic forms to be inherently inadequate and looks upon the space of democratic speech and representation as a travesty of a truth which some would seek to hide and others seek to hide from themselves.

The practice of democracy has thus found itself dogged by an attitude of suspicion, of *looking underneath*, which relates all democratic statements to a concealed truth of inequality, exploitation or splitting. Two themes have been combined: that of formal democracy as opposed to real democracy, and that of the illusion peculiar to the spontaneous consciousness of social actors – and most specifically the spontaneous consciousness of the exploited, who are separated from the meaning of their own practice. Whence a discourse with two main features: a dogmatism based on the idea of a hidden truth and a scepticism based on the idea that misapprehension is inevitable. This theoretical apparatus has demonstrated the formidable power to survive the collapse of its political models. Precisely where the great models of political hope are in ruins, at a time when one no longer dares propose any rival to democracy as the good form of collective life, dogmatism has effectively outlived itself in the guise of scepticism. The indeterminate ritual of demystification continues to impose a way of thinking (and practising) democracy on the basis of suspicion, as if it always had to be made to confess that it is not what it claims to be, and that those who practise it are perpetually deluded about what they are doing.

This view of things has ended up so obscuring the very meaning of the socialist experience, and in particular the meaning of the working-class socialist experience, that this experience is now mistaken for an achievement of democracy. This is what I should like to demonstrate by examining some aspects of what I shall call the *vita democratica* – rather as Hannah Arendt speaks of the *vita activa*. I shall deal with just two such aspects in what follows: the *use of words* and the *use of forms*.

2. The Use of Words and the Syllogism of Emancipation

First let us consider the history of one particular idea and practice in nineteenth-century France – the idea and practice of workers' emancipation. As a matter of fact, this idea established itself by virtue of a whole system of discourses and practices which completely rejected any notion of hidden truth and its demystification. Seen in this light, the experience of working-class militancy takes on an aspect quite different from the one we are accustomed to: it becomes a sort of testing of equality. Social science has of course always concerned itself essentially with one thing, proving the existence of inequality. And indeed in this endeavour it has been highly successful. But the fact that the science of social criticism is perpetually rediscovering inequality is to my mind precisely what makes it worth taking another look at the practices which set out to do just the opposite. We may well be led in this way to ask who is the more naive, those who demonstrate the existence of inequality or those who demonstrate the existence of equality – and indeed whether the idea of naivety itself has any pertinence here.

The aftermath of the revolution of 1830 in France saw an efflorescence of working-class publications, pamphlets and newspapers all basically asking the same question: are the French people equals or are they not? These texts, which often go hand in hand with strike movements or other kinds of movements, tend to take the approximate form of a syllogism.

The major premiss of this syllogism is simple: the Charter promulgated in 1830 says in its preamble that all French people are equal before the law, and this equality constitutes the syllogism's major premiss. The minor premiss is derived rather from direct experience. For example, in 1833, workers in the Paris tailoring trade went on strike because the master tailors refused to respond to their demands relating to rates of pay, working hours and working conditions. Here, then, the minor premiss would run something like this: now Monsieur Schwartz, the head of the master tailors' association, refuses to listen to our case. What we are putting to him is a case for revised rates of pay. He can verify this case but he refuses to do so. He is therefore not treating us as equals. And he is therefore contradicting the equality inscribed in the Charter.

Here is another form of the syllogism: the same Monsieur Schwartz meets with his colleagues and reaches an agreement with them to resist the workers' demands. So he organizes a bosses' federation. Now, the law says that masters' federations are to be condemned by the same token as those of the workers. Yet only the workers are prosecuted. Here too equality is contradicted.

Another contemporary example: the law says that French people are equal, yet Monsieur Persil, Public Prosecutor to the King, has just said, in his indictment against a town crier:

> Everything which the Law has done against press licence and against political associations would be lost if *workers* were daily to be given a picture of their position, by comparison with a more elevated class of men in society, by repeated assurances that they are *men just like those others*, and that they have a right to enjoy the same things.

Here then is a new minor premiss of the syllogism: a representative of the law who has just said that workers are not like other men.

The syllogism is simple: the major premiss contains what the law has to say; the minor, what is said or done elsewhere, any word or deed which contradicts the fundamental legal/political affirmation of equality.

But there are two ways of conceiving the contradiction between the major and minor premisses. The first is the way to which we are accustomed. It amounts to the simple conclusion that the legal/political words are illusory, that the equality asserted is merely a façade designed to mask the reality of inequality.

Thus reasons the good sense of demystification. Yet this is by no means the logic followed by these workers. The conclusion they draw is usually that either the minor premiss or the major must be changed. If Monsieur Persil or Monsieur Schwartz is right to say what he says and do what he does, the preamble of the Charter must be deleted. It should read: the French people are not equal. If, by contrast, the major premiss is upheld, then Monsieur Persil or Monsieur Schwartz must speak or act differently.

The interesting thing about this way of reasoning is that it no longer opposes word to deed or form to reality. It opposes word to word and deed to deed. Taking what is usually thought of as something to be dismissed, as a groundless claim, it transforms it into its opposite – into the grounds for a claim, into a space open to dispute. The evocation of equality is thus not *nothing*. A word has all the power originally given it. This power is in the first place the power to create a space where equality can state its own claim: equality exists somewhere; it is spoken of and written about. It must therefore be verifiable. Here is the basis for a practice that sets itself the task of verifying this equality.

How can one verify words? Essentially, through one's actions. These actions must be organized like a proof, a system of reasons. In our example, this approach entails a determining transformation in the practice of the strike. The strike takes on the form of a logical proof. Previously, the refusal of work had been caught up in the logic of a power struggle culminating in what journeymen called a 'damnation': when they were dissatisfied with the employers of a town, they 'damned' the town, that is to say they left with bag and baggage, and sought to prevent anyone else from replacing them. Against this logic of outright rejection the new practice of the strike strove to transform an alignment of forces into a logical confrontation. This did not simply mean substituting words for actions; rather, it meant transforming a power relationship by means of a practice of logical demonstration.

What had to be demonstrated was, precisely, equality. The tailors' strike demands in 1833 included a formulation which seems strange: they asked for 'relations of equality' with the masters. This may appear naive or peculiar to us, but the sense of the thing is clear: there are workers and there are masters, but the masters are not the masters of their workers. In other words, two sets of relations have to be reckoned with. On the one hand, a relation of economic dependence exists which engenders a particular social reality – a particular distribution of roles, as echoed in the everyday order of working conditions and personal relationships. This 'social' reality is a reality of inequality. On the other hand, a legal/political relation exists: the inscription of equality, as it appears in the founding texts, from the Declaration of the Rights of Man to the preamble of the Charter. This second relation has the force to engender a different social reality, one founded on equality; in this case what this means is making negotiation a customary thing; it also means imposing particular rules of courtesy on the masters or establishing the workers' right to read the newspaper in the workshop. This *social* equality is neither a simple legal/political equality nor an economic levelling. It is an equality enshrined as a potentiality in legal/political texts, then translated, displaced and maximized in everyday life. Nor is it the whole of equality: it is a way of living out the relation between equality and inequality, of living it and at the same time displacing it in a positive way.

This is the definition of a struggle for equality which can never be merely a demand upon the other, nor a pressure put upon him, but always simultaneously a proof given to oneself. This is what 'emancipation' means. It means escaping from a minority. But nobody escapes from the social minority save by their own efforts. The emancipation of the workers is not a matter of making labour the founding principle of the new society, but rather of the workers emerging from their minority status and proving that they truly belong to the society, that they truly communicate with all in a common space; that they are not merely creatures of need, of complaint and protest, but creatures of discourse and reason, that they are capable of opposing reason with reason and of giving their action a demonstrative form. Thus, the particular strike we have been considering was constructed as a set of arguments: the tailors' demonstration of the fairness of the pay increases demanded, their commentary on the texts of their adversaries in order to prove their irrationality, the economic organization of the strike through the creation of a workshop managed by the workers themselves – this less as a germ of some 'workers' power' to come than as an extension of the republican principle to a realm still foreign to it, namely the workshop. Perhaps after all there is no need for the workers to own their own factory and run it themselves in order to be equal. Perhaps it is enough for them to show, when appropriate, that they *can* do so. Not to found a counterpower susceptible of governing a future society, but simply to effect a demonstration of *capacity* which is also a demonstration of *community*. Self-emancipation is not secession, but self-affirmation as a joint-sharer in a common world, with the assumption, appearances to the contrary notwithstanding, that one can play the same game as the adversary. Whence the proliferation in the literature of workers' emancipation – as also in that of women's emancipation – of arguments aiming to prove that those demanding equality have a perfect right to it, that they participate in a common world where they can prove their case and prove the necessity for the other to recognize it.

Of course, proving one is correct has never compelled others to recognize they are wrong. In order to uphold one's correctness other kinds of arguments have always been needed. The affirmation of the right to be correct is dependent on the violence of its inscription. Thus, the reasonable arguments of the strikers of 1833 were audible, their demonstration visible, only because the events of 1830, recalling those of 1789, had torn them from the nether world of inarticulate sounds and ensconced them by a contingent forced-entry in the world of meaning and visibility. The repetition of egalitarian words is a repetition of that forced-entry, which is why the space of shared meaning it opens up is not a space of consensus. Democracy is the community of sharing, in both senses of the term: a membership in a single world which can only be expressed in adversarial terms, and a coming together which can only occur in conflict. To postulate a world of shared meaning is always transgressive. It assumes a symbolic violence both in respect of the other and in respect of oneself. The legitimate subject which no text is adequate to found exists only in the act of this double violence. Proving to the other that there is only one world and that one can prove the legitimacy of one's action within it, means first of all proving this to oneself. Hannah Arendt posits as the primary right the right to have rights. We might add that rights are held by those who can impose a rational obligation on the other to recognize them. That the other more often than not evades such obligations changes the problem in no essential way. Those who say on general grounds that the other cannot understand them, that there is no common language, lose any basis for rights of their own to be recognized. By contrast, those who act as though the other can always understand their arguments increase their own strength – and not merely at the level of argument. The existence of a subject in law implies that the legal words are verifiable within a sphere of shared meaning. This space is virtual, which is not to say illusory. Those who take the virtual for the illusory disarm themselves just like those who take the community of sharing for a community of consensus. The call for equality never makes itself heard without defining its own space. The narrow path of emancipation passes between an acceptance of separate worlds and the illusion of consensus. It is this tension which is caricatured by analyses that oppose the formal to the real or by second thoughts which exchange one position for its opposite. Analyses of the day before, which contrast real liberty and equality with their formal declaration, and analyses of the day after, which contrast the good, decorous revolutions of liberty with the utopian and murderous revolutions of equality, both overlook the same thing: equality and liberty are forces engendered and augmented by their own actualization. And this is what the idea of emancipation implies when it asserts that there is no such thing as illusory liberty or illusory equality, that both are real forces whose actual effects need to be verified.

This also implies that there is no group strength independent of the strength with which individuals tear themselves out of the nether world of inarticulate sounds and assert themselves as sharers in a common world. Thus, the idea of emancipation has made its way forward through a multitude of individual experiences. I have had occasion to study the records of one of those countless singular experiences, that of a worker who created for himself an entire ethic, even an economy, of emancipation: a whole system for measuring freedom, a sort of counterpolitical economy whereby, in every act of daily life, it became possible to assess the acquisition, not of the greatest amount of goods, but of the greatest amount of freedom.[3] In this way, he invented a style of living based on having fewer and fewer needs and continually exchanging them for freedom. It would be interesting to compare this ascetic economy – a 'cenobitic' economy, he called it – with present-day theories of the individual agent and 'cost analyses' applied to the individual. Such a comparison would show how individual emancipation carried to its logical extreme reconnects with shared concerns. Thus, one of my 'plebeian philosopher''s essential budget headings was 'shoes', for the emancipated man is a man who walks and walks, moving around and conversing, putting meaning into circulation and promoting the movement of emancipation. On the one hand, the emancipation of the worker entails a change in his style of living, an aestheticization of his life. On the other, the point where man meets citizen, where the individual working out his own life by calculation becomes a member of the community, is located in the fact that man is first of all a creature who speaks: it is essentially as a speaking being that he discovers his equality with all other human beings. Indeed, it is thanks to theorists of language that, in France, the word emancipation has taken on a new meaning, transcending its legal sense, and come to connote a new individual and collective experience. At the heart of this new idea of emancipation is the notion of equality of intelligences as the common prerequisite of both intelligibility and community, as a presupposition which everyone must strive to validate on their own account.[4]

The democratic experience is thus one of a particular aesthetic of politics. The democratic man is a being who speaks, which is also to say a poetic being, a being capable of embracing a distance between words and things which is not deception, not trickery, but humanity; a being capable of embracing the unreality of representation. A poetic virtue, then, and a virtue grounded in trust. This means starting from the point of view of equality, asserting equality, assuming equality as a given, working out from equality, trying to see how productive it can be and thus maximizing all possible liberty and equality. By contrast, anyone who starts out from distrust, who assumes inequality and proposes to reduce it, can only succeed in setting up a hierarchy of inequalities, a hierarchy of priorities, a hierarchy of intelligences – and will reproduce inequality ad infinitum.

3. The Use of Forms

The same set of interpretations – and, I believe, of their effects – is revealed when we turn our attention to that other essential aspect of democratic life, the way in which forms are used. This may be clearly seen if we examine one of the cardinal forms of mediation between individuals and the political system in modern societies: the form of the school. The school is a privileged site for voicing suspicion concerning the non-truth of democracy and criticizing the gap between the form of democracy and its reality. Critical thinking about democratic education has highlighted one basic theme, that of failure; the failure *at* school of a large majority of children from working-class backgrounds has been taken as evidence of the failure *of* school to fulfil its task – the achievement of social equality.

The democratic school is thus regarded as a place where a promise is continually being broken, and here once again we encounter the double-barrelled approach of social criticism: the first target is failure, for which various remedies, pedagogical, psychological or sociological, are proposed; but no sooner is this target hit than a second is revealed, for to prove failure is also, and most of all, to prove that democracy is lying to itself, that it is ill adapted to the equality which it proclaims, that, on the sly, it is perfectly adapted to the inequality which it dissimulates and indeed that inequality is its true fundamental principle. The work of Bourdieu and Passeron exemplifies this logic, in which the sociologist and the social critic win every round by showing that democracy loses every round. What they set out to show is precisely that if the school has not fulfilled its egalitarian promises this is not for want of means but by virtue of its very mode of being and of the symbolic logic which is its foundation.[5] A book such as *The Inheritors* sets in motion in exemplary fashion what I shall call the syllogism of suspicion. This syllogism does not merely oppose a major premiss (the school as equal for all) to a minor one (the failure of working-class children) in order to produce an indictment. It is intended to show further that school creates inequality precisely because it promotes belief in equality; in having the children of the poor believe that all who are there are equal, that pupils are marked, classified and selected only on the basis of the talents and intelligence each has, it compels the children of the poor to acknowledge that if they do not succeed it is because they have no talents and are not intelligent, and it would therefore be better if they went somewhere else. The school thus becomes the theatre of a fundamental symbolic violence which is nothing but the very illusion of equality. In order to convince that success is linked only to the talents of the pupil, the school privileges everything which goes beyond the simple transfer of knowledge, everything which is supposed to call upon the personality and originality of the pupil. In doing this it selects a mode of being which is in reality a style of life, a form of acculturation which is not learnt at school – that of the 'inheritors'. It thus reveals itself as false to its promise and faithful to its hidden essence: the Greek *schole*, which gave school its name and whose initial meaning is the condition of persons of leisure, who as such are equal and able on account of their social privilege to devote themselves, should they so desire, to study.

Thus, the form of the school describes a perfect circle: the conversion of socio-economic capital into cultural capital, and, thanks to the practical dissimulation of this conversion, which is as invisible as it is effective, a separation of those who have from those who do not have the means to effect it. More broadly, the democratic form nourishes both the illusion of equality and the misapprehension of a basic inequality – the inequality between the leisure of the *schole* and the realm of necessity, between those who can and those who cannot afford the luxury of the symbolic. Democracy is a fraudulent regime which presumes that luxury is a possibility for the poor. This is the ultimate logic of the argument of suspicion, which makes democratic man a man abused by the forms whereby division is at once perpetuated and disguised.

True, this nihilistic interpretation of the argument of suspicion is countered by a positive political interpretation based on the 'reduction of inequalities'. This account is proffered by reformist pedagogues and politicians who essentially retain three ideas from Bourdieu and Passeron's critique: the necessity to make explicit the factors implicit in inequality, to struggle against the formalism of the dominant culture and to take into account the weight of the social, of the *habitus* and modes of socialization characteristic of the disadvantaged classes. The outcome of these policies, in France at least, is now barely contested: supposed efforts to make inequality explicit have rigidified it. For one thing, the making explicit of sociocultural difference has tended to turn that difference into destiny and the institution of the school into an institution of assistance, with all that that entails in terms of reorientations and reclassifications serving to channel the children of immigrants away from any possible risk of failure. Meanwhile, the hunt for 'implicit' criteria has only aggravated the impact of the most explicit, as witness the mad race (which begins at nursery school level and is quickly internalized by the children) for a good primary school which will lead to a good junior school, thus paving the way to a good class in a good *lycée* located in a good sociocultural environment of a good area of the capital and so forth.

Thus, the nihilistic vision of school as a form of reproduction of inequality and the progressive vision of school as an instrument for reducing inequalities concur in their effects as they do in their principles: both start with inequality and end up with inequality. In asking for an education adapted to working-class needs, or denouncing an education that reproduces the domination of the workers, they reassert a monolithic presumption bequeathed by the counterrevolutionary critique of democracy to its socialist demystifiers: the idea that disharmony between the constitutive forms of a sociopolitical regime signifies an ill or a fundamental lie. Yet this is precisely the distinguishing feature of modern democracy: the heterogeneity of its forms, and here specifically the nonconvergence of the logic of schooling with the logic of production.

In one sense it is certainly true that democratic education is the paradoxical heir of the aristocratic *schole*, for it equalizes less by virtue of the universality of the knowledge it imparts, or by virtue of social levelling, than by virtue of its very form, which is that of a separation from productive life. From ancient hierarchical societies democracy borrows this form, which separates intellectual leisure and productive necessity. But out of this once natural separation it creates a contradiction in motion in which a variety of egalitarian policies are overlaid, encountering in frequently unpredictable guises the diverse ideological and social input of the users (that is to say, families). The ambiguity of the school's form opens it up to a multiplicity of choices and meanings: for some it is the realization of equal citizenship, for others a means to social mobility, and for yet others a right, independent of its actual use, be it successful or otherwise – a right which democracy owes to itself and to the wishes of its members, however indeterminate these may be. Most of the time all of these meanings mingle, making education neither the mask of inequality nor the instrument of inequality's reduction, but the site of a permanent negotiation of equality between the democratic state and the democratic individual: a manifold negotiation which, to unequal and often contradictory expectations, offers gains and losses which are infinitely more complex than those conceived of by the analysts of educational 'failure'.

Let me take one example from French politics. November 1986 saw the outbreak of a quite puzzling student strike against proposed government legislation on the universities. The basic aim of this legislation was to make higher education more responsive to economic requirements. One graduate in three, we were told, was unemployed. Hence the need to introduce a 'selective orientation' which would set students on the right path and match their abilities with eventual employment. (Another factor, I believe, was that the forces supporting the conservative majority like the word '*sélection*' for its own sake.) But the legislation before Parliament was very circumspect: a little selective orientation, but not too much; the universities would be allowed to increase enrolment fees, but not by too much either. This rather tepid law seemed destined to go through without a murmur of protest. Yet, within days, two hundred thousand students and *lycéens* were out on the streets of Paris demanding its rejection.

This movement was startling for a variety of reasons. Everything took place as if, despite the modesty of the legislation, the interested parties had taken in one word only, a word which was intolerable *per se*: 'selection'. Yet the context of this response contained no remnant of cultural revolution, and all the great debates challenging the capitalist education system had long since evaporated. The students and *lycéens* opposing the new law were themselves for the most part individually caught up in the logic of selection, in the search for good classes and good networks. This change in practical beliefs and attitudes seemingly posed no obstacle to the unyielding maintenance of a system of collective identification whereby a free and open university system was considered a hard-won and inalienable right of French democracy: a university where anyone can study anything, whatever the risks and potential losses for the individual and for the state – in short, a knowledge bazaar, to go back to the Platonic image – was evidently considered the due of the collectivity and of each of its members. That individuals should be entitled to the full scope of university education from the state, whether or not this leads to employment, is part of the negotiation of equality between the democratic state and democratic individuals. But this should not be taken to mean simply that the disordered wishes and calculations of the democratic bazaar force compromise on the administrators of the collective rationality. Democracy would indeed amount to no more than what Plato saw in it if it were simply the disorder of domination, the disharmony between its forms. The compromises and disorders of domination are only 'democratic' to the extent that they themselves are effects of egalitarian division, the contingent historical configurations where that division can recognize its own place and reaffirm its power, which is the power to declassify. For this is exactly what is at stake in the word 'selection', which some take pleasure merely in uttering and others refuse even to hear. The seemingly apolitical young people who took to the streets to contest this single word appear to have grasped its meaning well; the issue came down to equality versus inequality, a simple matter of knowing which of the two in the final instance ruled over the democratic compromise and gave it its meaning: the rights of the multitude or the rights of the administrators of the *ochlos* in all their wisdom.

Which gives us some perspective, it seems to me, on the contradictory assessments that were made of this calm, lukewarm and apparently unromantic movement. There were those who hailed the realism of young people who, unlike the revolutionaries of 1968, were able clearly to define their objectives and peacefully organize their troops. Others, on the contrary, attacked the pettiness of a movement fixated on immediate interests and ludicrously concerned with respectability. But perhaps both these views miss one of the most remarkable aspects of what one calls realism and the other reformism. For something truly remarkable happened in this movement. Copies of the proposed legislation were massively distributed throughout the universities. The students bought it, read it and discussed it. In our day, we did not read the text of proposed legislation on the universities. We knew what they expressed: the submission of the university to capitalist power. We had nothing to say to the politicians who proposed them, except that capitalism spoke out of their mouths and that they could do nothing other than what they *were* doing. For their part they expected no other reaction from us and accordingly had no problems besides that of maintaining order. This time, though, something took place which created total disarray in the ranks of the government and the majority: the students evaluated the law and pronounced it a bad law. They addressed the politicians as if they were people who could, after all, just as easily make good laws as bad ones. Politicians expecting the usual refrain, 'Capitalism speaks out of your mouths', suddenly found themselves being taken seriously as legislators, being treated as if they could perfectly well make laws in the general interest, since that was what they had been elected for. This 'naivety' of the students of 1986, whose reasoning resembled that of the striking tailors of 1833, enabled them, by playing the others' game, to create a quite new polemical space, taking their interlocutors completely by surprise and leaving them nonplussed – caught, in fact, in the trap of the reinvented syllogism of equality.

The force of this syllogism, however, by no means reposes on the superiority of realism over utopia, or of peaceful over violent methods. It is not a characteristic of the syllogism of equality that it replaces strife by talk. Rather, it establishes a common space as a space of division. Transcending the decline of the great figures of class struggle and revolutionary hope, the modesty of the 1986 demonstrators touched the same sensitive point as the violence of the *enragés* of 1968. It asserted the strength of the dividing many against the consensual – and ochlocratic – degeneracy of democracy: against government by well-selected elites in the name of a harmonious management of the scattered desires of the mass. Against the hierarchies of consensus and the passions of exclusion, the occupation of the street by the anonymous multitude reaffirms the community of sharing. And this it can do only by tracing that violent inscription which made the contingent site of the negotiation of knowledge into a place for the exercise of egalitarian transgression.

4. Democracy Now

I have considered two instances of democratic practice, one taken from the heroic age of a combative democracy, the other from the ambiguous age of a democracy which in the very banalization of its rule, of its self-regulation, allows us to glimpse the outline of its involution. It seems to me that these two examples shed a new light on certain contemporary analyses of the phenomenon of democracy.

I am thinking in the first place of the vision encapsulated by Jean-François Lyotard in the idea of postmodernity. After the age of grand narratives of the social, centred on the theme of the absolute wrong and the universal victim, democratic indeterminacy has turned out, according to Lyotard, to be synonymous in principle with that 'insistent pressure of the infinite on the will' which characterizes the infinite tumult of capital.[6] The logic of capital tends always to create discordance, heterogeneity between linguistic discourses. This heterogeneity prohibits the discourse of the universal victim but allows the same experience to be phrased in an infinity of different ways; thus working-class experience may be variously articulated in the language of contractual negotiations or in that of discourse on the subject of Labour.

This approach has the merit of abolishing the distance that suspicion maintains, but it does so from the starting-point of the categories of suspicion themselves. Just as, for Marx, bourgeois progressivism dissipated the illusion of chivalry, so, for Lyotard, the democracy of capital dissipates the proletarian illusion. With the collapse of the political fantasy of the One, what asserts itself, in its positivity, is solely the economic tumult of difference, which is called, without distinction, either capital or democracy. More generally, Lyotard evokes a positive aspect for the various forms of suspicion regarding democracy.

He thus inverts the Platonic condemnation of indeterminacy, of the democratic *apeiron*, ascribing a positive value to the theme of democracy as a bazaar. Likewise, he reverses the usual interpretation of the contemporary themes of the 'end of ideology' or of 'depoliticization' in advanced democratic societies. Yet this upside-down Platonism surely fails to break out of the Platonic mould and continues to identify the democratic *apeiron* with nothing more than the turbulence of appetites, even if this makes two readings possible: an exoteric reading which stops short at the narcissistic self-gratification of the 'pluralist' society, or an esoteric reading which reopens the infinite gap between the Republic and democracy, seeing the rule of administrative rationality as a 'soft' form of totalitarianism. When all is said and done, does not such an approach fail to grasp all the current complexity of the democratic phenomenon? For example, what made the French students' strike so strange was the durability of certain identifications in the very midst of the rout of all the great incorporations, the recognition of a *wrong* even in the absence of a victim. In a situation where the demands of economic competition and geopolitical equilibrium now leave democracies the slenderest of margins for political alternatives, where individual ways of assessing life refer to broadly consensual values, suddenly it takes almost nothing – one word too many, say – for a polemical space to re-emerge where trivial differences are translated into major options, where a system of possibilities with the minutest of variables gives way to a basic alternative in which a choice has to be made between egalitarian words which confirm democracy and inegalitarian words which contradict it. Litigation generally continues to rule in politics. Where it no longer holds sway, it is not the postmodern logic of disjunction which manifests itself, but the return of the archaic: straightforward brutality in its diverse guises, from the alleged language of numbers to the all too real howls of the hate-filled pack, effectively resuscitating the victim as the unnameable, as a stranger to the law of discourse. The apparent logic of post-modernity thus explodes between two 'archaisms'. Faced with the return of the animalistic aspect of politics, the democratic virtue of trust recreates a polemical space of shared meaning. This is, precisely, the strength of equality, which acts through those small differences that can give a radically different sense to the same experience. I have no hesitation in saying that what is happening here is (to stay with the Platonic lexicon) of the order of *reminiscence*. Suddenly, in the very slumber of political discourse, equality appears as the thing that gives a common meaning to the infinite variety of 'selfish' individual uses of a democratic form.

To many this reminiscence seems too evanescent. In their view, it needs to be given solidity. This is the meaning of that other analysis of contemporary democracy which is primarily expressed through the theme of participation. Yet I wonder whether this notion, offered as a solution to the problems of democracy, is not rather a solution to the problems of the critique of democracy – the small change of fallen grand alternatives. The idea of participation blends two ideas of different origins: the reformist idea of necessary mediations between the centre and the periphery, and the revolutionary idea of the permanent involvement of citizen-subjects in every domain. The mixture of the two produces this mongrel idea, assigning to enduring democracy, as its site of exercise, the mere filling of spaces left empty by power. But does not the permanence of democracy reside much rather in its mobility, its capacity to shift the sites and forms of participation? When striking workers acquire power by demonstrating that they can, if need be, run their own factory, why should we wish for that power to find its permanent expression there on the spot, in the form of self-management? Likewise, during the student strike, one heard remarks such as the following: 'There ought to have been a preliminary dialogue between the interested parties'. But this is an entirely retrospective argument: there simply was no interlocutor for the consultation which 'should have' taken place *before* the birth of this ephemeral power. Genuine participation is the invention of that unpredictable subject which momentarily occupies the street, the invention of a movement born of nothing but democracy itself. The guarantee of permanent democracy is not the filling up of all the dead times and empty spaces by the forms of participation or of counterpower; it is the continual renewal of the actors and of the forms of their actions, the ever-open possibility of the fresh emergence of this fleeting subject. The test of democracy must ever be in democracy's own image: versatile, sporadic – and founded on trust.

Notes

1   C.B. Macpherson, *The Life and Times of Liberal Democracy*, Oxford 1977.
2   See Aristotle, *Politics*, IV, 1294b, 35–6.
3   See Gabriel Gauny, *Le philosophe plébéien*, writings collected and edited by Jacques Rancière, Paris 1983.
4   See Jacques Rancière, *Le maître ignorant*, Paris 1987; also, in this volume, 'The Community of Equals', Chapter 3.
5   See Pierre Bourdieu and Jean-Claude Passeron, *Les héritiers, les étudiants et la culture*, Paris 1964, translated as *The Inheritors: French Students and Their Relations to Culture*, Chicago 1979; and Bourdieu and Passeron, *La reproduction, Eléments pour une théorie du système d'enseignement*, translated as *Reproduction in Education, Society and Culture*, London 1977. I view the theses of Bourdieu and Passeron at the level of generality at which they have obtained their success within the political doxies, and independently of the subsequent development of either author.
6   See Lyotard's *Tombeau de l'intellectuel et autres papiers*, Paris 1984. Here again I am singling out theses which were perhaps able to systematize the thinking of a specific moment in time. It is worth noting, however, that Lyotard's subsequent work has continued relentlessly to undermine any optimistic reading of postmodernity.

3

The Community of Equals

The theme of the community of equals nowadays generally gives rise to two kinds of brooding. The first is a grudging relief. There is an entire literature that invites us to shudder retrospectively at the thought of the danger we were in (or would have been in if we had not been so smart) from the combined threat of real levelling on the one hand and the great Whole which swallows up individual will and reason on the other. A somewhat degenerate form of catharsis is the justification given for such literary endeavours, which see fit to set continually before our eyes the fantasy of that great entity whose fascination for us so clearly spelt our doom. The second kind of brooding is a 'reasonable' nostalgia. Though only too well aware of what the above-mentioned threat made possible, we still take it to represent something we would not want to lose, namely a particular configuration of being-together without which thought and action are bereft of the virtue of generosity which distinguishes the political from mere business management. By some inverse exorcism, it is the very *passé* and superseded character of this figure, which is no longer the object of either fear or hope, that serves to maintain that barely perceptible gap and allows a shimmering cloud of egalitarian and communal honour to continue hovering above the banal administration of financial indexes and corporate reorganizations.

Both these feelings gauge a conceptual figure by the balance sheet of history. If we want to avoid this, perhaps we need to alter the terms of the question slightly; perhaps, instead of settling our accounts with the community of equals, we ought to consider how the community of equals does its own accounting, or rather what kind of accounting gives rise to this figure in the first place. What I have in mind here is a twofold line of inquiry. The more fundamental aspect – which I shall leave aside for now – has to do with the relationship of the idea of community to the idea of loss itself, to what we retain of a loss or to what takes shape around it. In this connection, I am put in mind of a quatrain of Rilke's which reminds us that 'Losing too is ours' (*Auch noch verlieren ist unser*), thus linking the notion of loss to the notion of common property. Even more simply, we might well recall the link between the idea of community and the judgement of the Gospel according to which 'He that findeth his life shall lose it' – a pronouncement which may readily be coupled with the Platonic motif of the inversion of life, and which has the following remarkable implication: the collapse of the representation of another life does not nullify that life but instead lends it a vertiginous reality. And at the core of this vertiginousness is equality, the desire to partake of equality.

I shall leave aside this basic or overarching question, however, and concentrate on an issue that arises from it. The fact is that the great accounting between the Whole and loss breaks down into a series of smaller calculations, into ways of measuring equality that do not allow themselves to be reduced to rules and standards without putting up a fight. Ways of counting, of counting oneself, of getting oneself to count. Ways of defining interests that cannot be reduced even to the simple calculation of pleasure versus pain; forms of profit that are also ways of being-together (of resembling one another or being distinct from one another) and of defining those gaps which Hannah Arendt saw as the very principle of political *inter esse*. And ways of defining interests entered on more lines and in more ledgers than can be covered by the double bookkeeping of reality/utopia and science/ideology. Our inquiry needs therefore to go into a lower gear: whenever equality or community is the issue, we need to ask what is in a position to win or lose a particular interest on such and such a line. In how many ways may equals be reckoned equal? How indeed are they to be counted in order for this calculation to be made? And so on.

If we pursue a few of these accountings, we shall be led to reconsider the notion that the standard of equality is the law (whether celestial or infernal) of the communitarian body. For it may well be that relations of community and equality are themselves but a never-ending settling of accounts. By taking a closer look at the accounts presented by equality to community we shall see the image of the single great body crumble, and encounter all the deficit and discord which ensure that the community of equals can never materialize without some cement plugging the cracks in the image, without some obligation to keep tallying members and ranks and retranslating the terms of the formula.

1. Concerning a Letter: The Banquet of Equals

As the starting-point of my analysis I shall borrow an example from one of the most significant configurations of communitarian thought, the one known, more or less adequately, as 'utopian socialism'. In 1838 Pierre Leroux published De l'Egalité, then in 1840 De l'Humanité – two works intent on founding the modern community of equals on a tradition as long as human history and mobilizing to this end both the laws of Moses and the law of Minos, the city of the ancients and the Fathers of the Church. Leroux's thesis is presided over by a master image, that of the fraternal meal, and a master text, the words of the Epistle to the Romans which teach that, as one body in Christ, we are all members one of the other.[1] Image and text were perfectly appropriate to the period, for they perfectly symbolized socialist and communist ardour – and the working-class press, both socialist and communist, copiously adopted Leroux's citations, if not his ideas; today they are appropriately horrifying, evoking as they do the spectre of the great all-devouring Whole. Seen in operation, however, this master image and this master formulation quickly betray their contradictions and impose the need for a reaccounting, a recementing, a rewriting.

Thus, in his exposition of the ancient tradition of the fraternal meal in De l'Egalité, Leroux encounters a curious philological problem. He analyses the establishment of this tradition in terms of its dual aspect, its dual origin: practices of warrior fraternity on the one hand and practices of periodic redistribution of wealth on the other, bringing together the Mosaic tradition and the Greek tradition in a continuous history culminating in the Essene community, which Leroux considered the origin of the founder of the Eucharist. Along the way, Leroux came across a problem of denomination which had already given pause to his inspiration, the Plutarch of the *Life of Lycurgus*. The fraternal meals of the Spartans were called *phidities*. Plutarch felt that they should properly be called *philities*, or meals of friendship, for the Greek *pheidein* means to economize – suggesting that fraternal meals were above all frugal. We know that the Spartans were considered miserly, and Plato recalled this in his portrait of the timocratic man. But Plutarch settled the issue, and Leroux followed suit: a lambda replaced a delta, and the Spartans' meals henceforward had a name that corresponded to their concept.

More is involved here, though, than mental convenience. Leroux does have a specific purpose, which is to identify the still fettered and only partially realized principle of an open community within a closed one. In the small Spartan brotherhood he seeks the principle of the great human community. He sees this aristocratic caste as the limited, one-sided realization of equality, a society of equals or friends founded on exclusion but perfect in itself; its forced closure is supposed to be the necessary and sufficient condition of the caste's transition to humanity. The caste must therefore be kept free from grasping timocracy, but this necessity causes Leroux to shun another line of thought, one stemming from that excised delta and susceptible of transporting us from Sparta to Athens, and from the relationship between aristocracy and timocracy to that between community and democracy.

Let me trace this other line of inquiry by way of a passage in Aristotle's *Rhetoric*, from the chapter on 'witticisms' (which are in the first place *asteia* – or things people say in the city). Aristotle refers in passing to a joke of Diogenes' which also involves a kind of political regime, table manners and the mode of being of a city. Diogenes, he tells us, said that the Athenians found their *phidities* in taverns.[2] In other words, the personal economies and collective equality sought by the Spartans in the institution of *phidities* were found by the Athenians in restaurants and public meeting-places. This is another way of setting up a contrast, as the Pericles of Thucydides does, between the Athenian school of freedom and easy living, and the military discipline of Spartan society. The anecdote naturally gains from being recounted by the theoretician of *philia* and political societies. And it will no doubt remind not a few readers of the place in the *Politics* where, making the case for democratic wisdom in opposition to the partisans of government by the wise, Aristotle employs another gastronomical argument. For the same cost, he tells us, you can eat better at communal meals where each pays an equal share. The same should go for political deliberations: the combined contributions of the many small Athenian intellects must always exceed in deliberative potential whatever the few scholarly intellects can together offer.[3]

So Leroux rejects an inconvenient delta and with it any consideration of equality's accounts with community. He decides to ignore the bite timocracy takes out of aristocracy and the bite democracy takes out of community. For, like timocracy for aristocracy, democracy is too avaricious for community. Democracy is what muddles community, what continually reduces it to its own messiness; it is the *unthinkable* aspect of community. Plato took it upon himself to think this unthinkable, this discordance between community and democracy. Our moderns in the main refuse to do so. Instead, they apportion things differently, they change letters, they overlay images. In this way, the modern political tradition has fashioned a strange model of fraternity as it was in the ancient world. By superimposing different pictures it allows us to envision a Spartan Athens or an Athenian Sparta: a more democratic and civilized Sparta, where fine speeches are made and dashing deeds done. This is how Rousseau's Sparta is fashioned, for example – or Leroux's. The same goes for the Athens of Hannah Arendt: witness the way she isolates a short extract from the speech made by Pericles in Thucydides while neglecting what is in fact the structuring dichotomy of the speech – that between Athenian 'freedom' and Spartan militarism.

This lets her set up an exemplary political stage where peers (*homoioi*) distinguish themselves by making the fine speeches and performing the fine deeds that confer a brilliant immortality upon the precariousness of human actions.

2. Concerning an Image: The Communitarian Body

Perhaps two Greeces are always needed to arrive at one Greece. Certainly the master image of the fraternal meal cannot be sustained otherwise. But the Christian formula and image of the fraternal body pose an identical problem. 'So we, being many, are one body in Christ', says the Apostle, 'and every one members one of another.' Popularized by Leroux, this formula was unproblematically annexed by the communists and provided *La Fraternité*, the leading working-class communist organ, with its masthead motto. Yet neither those who gave it pride of place nor those who even at the time denounced the great pantheistic Whole as a fantasy seem to have been aware of the exact Pauline context of the formulation. The image of the members of the body was nevertheless introduced by the Apostle in response to a quite specific issue, namely the distribution and hierarchy of charisms within the Christian community. The question of charisms was in effect that of the division of labour in a spiritual community. It was necessary for the gift of tongues and the gift of miracles, the gift of cures and the gift of prophecies, to relate to one another as do the members of the body, each playing its part and assisting or being subordinate to the others. But even from Saint Paul's text two rather different conclusions may be drawn, depending on the term considered. On the *members*, Paul says two things: that it is their function to give one another mutual assistance, but also that a kind of equality is established among them by means of reciprocal compensations. A compensatory honour devolves upon those who are inferior by nature and function, just as the more noble parts of the body are left naked while the shameful ones are covered. As for charisms, the Apostle asserted, much more summarily, that they were not all equally useful, not all equally worthy of being sought. A system of classification was called for, founded on the justness of the whole. But how was this justness to be understood? There were in fact two rival interpretations or glosses here. 'God', said the communist *La Fraternité*, 'arranged an order of this kind (of perfect equality) so that there might be no schism or division but that the members might offer one another mutual aid.'[4] In order thus to extract a communist image from the Christian one, however, this egalitarian commentary had to overlook the long tradition of the commentaries of the Church Fathers, a tradition which Gregory of Nazianzus sums up in a treatise bearing the unequivocal title 'On Well-Ordered Debate. That It Is Not Fitting for Every Man in Every Circumstance to Debate upon the Divinity': 'One part (*meros*) commands and presides. Another is led and directed. We may not all be the tongue, nor all prophets, apostles, interpreters, etc.'[5] The formula for equality is thus also the formula for ecclesiastical hierarchy.

This interpretative chiasma therefore reveals another superimposition of images: the image of the great Christlike communist body overlays the Pauline image of the body of the Church. But the latter is itself a superimposition, for behind the fable of the distribution of charisms may be discerned an older fable, an exemplary narrative of the division of labour in the social body: the fable of the belly and the limbs told by Menenius Agrippa to the plebeians after their withdrawal to the Aventine hill. Behind the image of the great Whole, then, the figure of division and recementing. But Menenius Agrippa's simple apologue achieves a formula for community only by leaving a double dilemma unresolved.

First of all, there was the problem of superiors. The senator-orator restored order in the revolt of the plebs by expounding a law of communal coexistence which was also a law of hierarchical subordination. Accordingly, the plebeians were the belly, the vegetative part of the city, powerless without the protection of the patricians' embrace. The trouble with this, however, was precisely the fact that he was compelled to tell this fable to the plebeians. The very principle of superiority collapses if it has to be explained to inferiors why they are inferior. This discourse assumes that it will be apprehended on its own terms, but the fact is that it portrays a community, governed by equality, which is quite different from the one that it promotes.

And the dilemma changes sides, so to speak, if the inferiors decide to adopt the apologue as their own, as a way of proclaiming their own equality. This is precisely what Leroux's contemporaries and the workers in *La Fraternité* did. They adopted the apologue and in the process inverted its identifications: they themselves became the active arms filling useless bellies. But this turning of the fable on its head exposes its mendacity: the hierarchy of functions it promotes is seen to conceal a pre-existent hierarchy of like and unlike. One enters the community of one's equals not by being useful to them but only by being like them. There is no way of being counted one of them without reflecting their own image: an equal is someone whose image is that of an equal. Making a virtue of usefulness, playing the card of function, is merely to preserve one's dissimilarity. No redistribution of members, functions or bodies can transform unlike into like. Another kind of likeness is required than the one that serves to close the caste of the *aristoi*.

3. The Community of Masters and the Community of Slaves

It will no doubt be objected that the egalitarian of 1840 had available quite a different model, one which Paul himself articulated for the benefit of the great human community, 'where there is neither Greek nor Jew, circumcision nor uncircumcision', but merely men all equally bearing the image of God. The trouble is that this new similitude puts a double twist on the similar, whereby what is gained is liable to be lost again immediately. The first stage of this twisting is the one that is applied to the very core of the communitarian paradigm represented by the community of the three divinities. Here, once again, the founding relationship of community hangs upon a single letter. Is the Son in the image of the Father? Or is he consubstantial with the Father? These two formulas are distinguished by virtue of a single iota, which puts a moat of blood between the heretics of resemblance (*homoiousia*) and the orthodox believers in consubstantiality (*homoousia*). The position of the orthodox believers is argued in the name of equality. To say that the Son is *like* the Father is to say that he is outside him, that he is not equal to him. But to posit the equality of Father and Son makes the Son into the Father's reflection. The unity of the Father and his image is thus asserted to be prior to any question of resemblance. Exemplary equals are not likes. But this first twist affirming equality at the expense of resemblance is immediately followed by a reverse one. In words borrowed from Saint Paul, Marius Victorinus sums up the radical becoming-other to which equality with the Father commits the Son, 'who did not regard his equality with the Father as a booty to be jealously guarded'.[6] The unity of the Father with his image prior to all question of resemblance is in fact worked out in the most radical dissimilarity, in that obedience unto death, unto death on the Cross, through which alone is made manifest the equality of will of Father and Son.

The formulation of Marius Victorinus, that equality is not a booty to be jealously guarded, has general force. Those whom the will of the Father and the sacrifice of the Son elevate or restore to the level of images of God are thereby 'delivered into slavery' to all their brothers. The double twisting of the like has daunting consequences for the Eucharistic fraternity which the new proclamation of the equality of likes is supposed to entail. The neat line of descent which is supposed to lead from the fraternal meal of the ancients to the Last Supper and the celebration of the Eucharist ignores the fact that the Eucharist is remarkably singular in the Christian conception of community. The basis of the early theory and practice of monastic communities – that is, communities of isolated men – is simply not the fraternity of the Eucharist nor the joy of brotherly sharing. The two canonical references to the Acts of the Apostles serve rather to remind those inclined to cheat over the giving up of their possessions about the punishment of Ananias. What these references are based on is obedience to the Cross. The fact is that the community of the servants of divine equality does not itself know equality. The glossary of the Rule of Saint Benedict is exemplary in this regard, for it notes but two uses of the adjective *aequalis* – the first to evoke the equality of the charity dispensed by an abbot to each of those who are entrusted to his care, and the second to empha-size the equality of the duty of obedience (*servitutis militium*) incumbent upon all monks. This does not reflect some normal-izing tendency within the monastic institution. The meaning assigned to obedience and the forms of its exercise may have var-ied, but from the rough discipline of the early fathers in the desert to the rule of the Benedictines, by way of the rule of Pachomius or the Institutions of John Cassian, one idea remained constant: the idea that obedience is not mere respect for a hier-archy but rather the general form of the relationship which servants of God must observe towards one another. In Saint Paul's words, to renounce self-will is to deliver onself up to oth-ers in slavery. In another commentary on the First Epistle to the Corinthians, Saint Basil the Great, in his 'Letter on the Perfection of the Lives of Monks', puts it thus: 'Thought and action should be as of one who has been delivered by God into slavery to his spiritual brothers (*homopsuchois adelphois*)'[7]; he adds, however, that each has his own particular rank (*en tagmati*). Saint Basil's 'Letter' deals with the application of this principle more particu-larly as it concerns the duties of young monks towards their elders, but the entirety of monastic practice and thought takes it as a more fundamental figure: the *homopsuchos* is a *homodou-los* – a companion in slavery. The community of monks, which is the Christian community par excellence, is made up not of equals but of men who are one another's slaves.

This figure would weigh heavy in the history of communitar-ian thought and practice. It appears inappropriate indeed as a basis for the grand fraternities of socialism or communism. And only too appropriate, on the other hand, to repetition in the guise of the sacrifice (or suicide) of the egalitarian militant who renounces his new-found emancipation in order to deliver himself into slavery to his brothers.

The paradox, then, is that at the moment when community of property came to be proposed as the way to realize equality, as the egalitarian solution to the 'social question', two great models of such community were available, but neither of them called for equality. What they did offer, strictly speaking, was either a community of masters or a community of slaves. In speaking of masters and slaves here, I am aware of forcing the symmetry somewhat, for this applies properly only to the second model, the monastic community of spiritual brothers dedicated to mutual slavery. By contrast, the first model, the communal paradigm par excellence, as outlined in Plato's *Republic*, of course presents not a community of masters but a community of guardians. The important point, though, is that the Platonic guardians are not equals either. Their community is founded not on property held in common but, on the contrary, on the fact that all they have of their own is what is common. The famous contrast between true (geometric) and false (arithmetical) equality implies that true equality, the equality of proportion, the one which merits the name of friendship, is established only through the wholesale rejection of the false variety, that of the citizen-artisans who place their claims to equality on the scales along with their merchandise. The community of guardians is in the first place the rejection of all affiliation or coaffiliation, of all forms of comparison or union between *single* individuals each having their own title to equality to advance in the assembly as in the marketplace. This community can only be understood in terms of the lack of possession, or more precisely the non-belonging to self, which is the corollary of mastery. Significant in this respect is the polemic in Book IV against the 'absurd' concept of self-mastery. Mastery is not thought but exercised. The strange notion of self-mastery has to be scaled back to its true meaning, which is the government of lower by higher, of the inferior by the best: of body by mind, of passions by intellect and of artisans by guardians. Properly, there is no such thing as a 'master of himself' – which is tantamount to saying that there are no equals. Only the well-ordered city itself answers to the category of *isotes*; it allows each individual to enjoy the benefits of its *isotes*. But it knows no equals and is itself equal to nothing, resembling only the divine model.

Strictly understood, the community of guardians ties non-belonging to inequality. The community is of masters or of slaves, and ultimately the two are equivalent. What is excluded here is the hybrid middle term, the equality of free subjects. The

Christian homologue of this Platonic polemic might well be seen in the peculiar rage which aroused Saint Basil the Great against those semi-Arians or disguised Arians who claimed that the Holy Spirit was neither master nor slave, but 'free'.[8] A choice had to be made, he insisted: either the Holy Spirit is a lord, partaking of the nature of the uncreated, or else a slave, partaking of the nature of the created. Since everything created was *homodoulos*, the Holy Spirit must therefore be a lord, but not, for all that, 'free', and can only belong to the community of the Master. As for the monks who obey the Master's will, we have seen that their community of ownership is simply the consequence of their non-possession of self. Which neatly sums up the answer of the Rule of Saint Benedict to the question whether monks should possess anything of their own: obviously not, since they are forbidden to possess either their own body or their own will.

4. Workers, Brothers, Communists

Thus, the two great models of community to which egalitarian thinking harked back in its golden age both posited a community that did not embrace equality. How was it, then, that this double admission of inequality was now reversed? To my mind the answer lies in the coming together of two ideas: an analysis of social division which saw this as the cause of inequality and the constitution of a new figure of equality itself. This analysis needed first of all to identify the principle of inequality with the selfish and asocial principle of separation. The basis of the reproduction of inequality was thus conflated with the principle of division which isolated individuals from one another. Division was selfish, and selfishness was divisive. Community therefore reinstituted equality to the extent that it instituted fraternity. All that remained was to define the identity of brothers in terms of their difference both from Plato's guardians and from the slaves of God. In order that brothers be neither masters nor slaves, the figure of the counterpart had to embody itself in a new social individuality having equality as its founding principle. Pierre Leroux sought to conceptualize this new individuality, to constitute a new anti-Platonic triad and to define the energy which

holds the members of an egalitarian humanity together. His contemporaries tended to mock his speculations. Like Socrates in
Book IV of the *Republic*, they took the view that this was going
a very long way round to find the principle of justice when it was
lying, so to speak, at one's feet. Socrates recognized this principle
in the rough wisdom of the division of labour; Leroux's contemporaries found it, for their part, in an undivided labour, in work
as a unitary principle. From their point of view, work presented
a double aspect. In the first place, it created identity. The same
certainty arose from moments of expansive cordiality, when the
refrain was 'We are all Workers', as from moments of conflict,
which pointed up the antagonism between toilers and idlers,
between real workers and loafers: the certainty that work was
now the generic name for human action as such. Second, the
identity thus created served as a measuring-rod: the figure of the
worker embodied the measure of work – the fact that work was
henceforward acknowledged as the source of goods and as the
measure of their value. If it had now become possible to forget
the hierarchical implications of the Platonic community or of the
Pauline fraternity, this was because the way work was measured
in the heyday of political economy had wiped out earlier fables
concerning the distribution of men and functions by imposing the
unitary law of the production and distribution of goods.

The idea of the community of fraternal workers could now be
formulated, and to this end three ideas were combined: first, an
arche of community, a single principle as to what the community
holds in common, namely workers, labour power and the prod-
ucts of labour; next, a precise measure which allows the principle
of fraternity immediately to become the principle of the distribution of functions and of the fruits of labour; and, last, the idea
of a virtue which can sustain the community and which is
embodied in a human figure. The fraternal worker is above all a
worker: the one who produces the material substance of what is
held in common keeps faith with the communal principle
through his daily activity.

In this way, an alliance is wrought between the principle of
political economy and the principle of fraternal community
under the banner of the equality of labour. The assumption

henceforward is that work which produces what is to be held in common is dedicated to solidarity, that in working for oneself one produces for others. The radical character of egalitarian communism resides in the extremely slender gap between this aspect of work in the glory days of political economy and the virtue of the communist worker's dedication to the cause of humanity. The trouble with the community of fraternal workers is that no sooner is it instituted than its system of identification collapses: the communist worker is immediately split into toiler and communist, worker and brother. A perfect instance of this dramatic development is supplied by the history of the community which Cabet took to the United States in order to found his communist Icaria. A curious article in the Icarian paper *Le Populaire* effectively summarizes the problem as experienced by the actors in the drama. Humanity, we are told, is comprised of but three kinds of people – workers, brothers and thieves. Workers and brothers will always manage to live together in one family. Thieves, however, have to be thrown out. And, the article concludes, the fraternal community is merely applying its own basic principle when it shows layabouts the door.[9]

Each term and each proposition here tend to open a gulf beneath the feet of this apparently simple reasoning. Let us confine ourselves for the moment to one simple question: who is the judge of the idleness that causes a poor worker to be identified as a thief? Is it the brother? Or is it not rather the worker, the only person equipped to transform 'less' work or 'less good' work into non-work or anti-work, that is to say into theft – a logical coup that might further be deemed a theft of fraternity. To put it another way, is not the word 'thief' here precisely a way of designating the intimate split between the worker and the brother? On the one hand, the brother assumes the face of the idler for whom the worker works; on the other, the worker assumes the face of the egotist who sacrifices brotherhood to work, to the income and enjoyment that work produces for him. A slogan echoing through the history of their community taught the Icarians that they had come in order to found Icaria, not in order to enjoy its fruits. But just who did the enjoying and who did the founding? What did the 'in order to' mean? And for whom?

Such questions were made more acute by the distribution of roles characteristic of the Icarian fraternity. First, there was the great family of French Icarian communists, then there was the vanguard detachment of Icarians who went ahead to found the communist colony in the United States, and last, the link between the two, 'Father' Cabet himself, epitomizing the law of fraternity and grounding the solidarity of the smaller community in the unity of the greater. This tripartite structure authorized endless permutations between the roles of founder and beneficiary, worker and brother, robber and robbed. On the one hand, those who left for America burnt their boats, abandoning their homeland and giving all they possessed to the community before setting off to found Icaria in the wilderness. Meanwhile, those who stayed in France stood to profit from the pioneers in two ways: in the first place, they enjoyed seeing their dream of fraternity fulfilled through the work of others, and second, if they followed, they would enjoy the fruits of the work of foundation directly. They would therefore always be in debt in the balance of foundation versus enjoyment. This relationship could also be viewed the other way round, however. Those who departed left behind the poverty and repression of the old world. Those who remained behind were left with the preoccupation of being communists and fraternal in a world of exploitation, and to continue finding enough work to subsidize their brothers in Icaria until such time as they had worked enough – and fraternally enough – to enjoy the material benefits of their labour. This reversible relationship of exploitation was further complicated when the founders wrote to their brothers in France and described the pleasures of Icaria to them. By doing so, they attracted the enthusiasm and financial support of potential new founders. When these converts duly arrived, the reality they encountered was not so bright as they had anticipated, and they were accused of having come merely to reap the rewards. To this reproach they retorted that they had come as founders and complained that those already reaping the rewards were the ones who had been abusing their fraternity in order to rob them. Such mutual recrimination could easily have gone on indefinitely. The truth of the matter, however, was not that some brothers were false. It was rather that work was unbrotherly and that the worker as worker had nothing to do with fraternity (which of course in no way prevented him, as a communist, from having a desperate love of it). The community of fraternal workers thus ends up splitting right down the middle into a party of work and a party of fraternity. In the Icarian case, the party of work was represented by the pioneers, who were aware of having 'delivered themselves into slavery' to their supposed brothers. Regarding themselves as exploited by the 'idleness' of the latter, they demanded more work and more equality. In opposition to them, the party of fraternity, embodied by 'Father' Cabet, denounced the egalitarian workers' lack of brotherliness as fermenting the destruction of the community. And why destroy the community, Cabet wanted to know, unless it be to share out the spoils and live at ease in a small community of workers, labouring much to benefit much, working not for the great human family but simply for themselves and their families. What Cabet discovered, without really thinking it through, was this: the communist worker was above all a sharer, and hence doubly determined (or doubly free of determination) as sharer giving and as sharer receiving. Though equality could always be represented as the fair distribution of shared efforts and shared rewards, in its essence it could never be anything but a continual tug of war over less and more which was only aggravated by the multiplicity of accounts demanding satisfaction. The equality specific to the fraternal community of workers was an endless balancing of debit and credit on the two lines of work and fraternity, the endless interchangeability of the roles of debtor and creditor. Discovering this, then, Cabet merely drew the conclusion that he had not sufficiently preached fraternity to his troops. The heart of the matter escaped him: the leap of logic constituted by the simple inference from labour-as-measure to the community of workers as the realization of justice. More of an orator than a philosopher, he failed to see that this was old Plato getting his revenge. Indeed, everything turned out just as though the failure of the Icarian community constituted a negative validation of the organizing principle of the Platonic city, that is to say, the radical separation between the action that defines the function of the guardians and the action that makes it possible to support them. If the guardians are to guard, the material preconditions of this support have to be produced entirely separately from them, entirely independent of their activity. It is not just that in a well-ordered city it is impossible to do more than one thing at a time. It is rather that this impossibility rests on a more fundamental principle – the principle that the community of guardians must be absolutely protected from the fluctuations of *more* and *less*, which together attach to material production and to the categories of mine and not-mine. The radical ill is this *apeiron*, the lack of determinacy of desire and the absence of limits on desire which stand opposed to any measuring of equality. This is precisely what is involved when it comes to the lack of equality in work. The measure of work is strictly correlated with the immeasurability of desire. There is simply no reason to subject oneself to equality in the measurement of work aside from that *more* which may be added to the worker's support. Every worker is an oligarch *in potentia*; every worker is a little capitalist.

Platonic radicalism here reveals how paradoxical it is to treat work, as producer and measure of wealth, as the logical basis of the worker as artisan of community. The realm of egalitarian workers is not the fraternal community but rather – to take another point of reference from the *Republic* – the hazy frontier betwen oligarchy and democracy, the singular moment when the principle of necessity and economy begins to vacillate in the indeterminacy of desires, where the desire of the worker's son for enjoyment begins to spread out across the multiplicity of objects of love. And let us not forget that equality, fraternity and community are also objects of love. Within community, the desire to enjoy the fruits of one's labour mingles in no precisely measurable way with the pleasures of egalitarian speech and of brotherly love, both of which may be embraced with sincerity to the point of suicide, or to the point of disillusionment or betrayal. Communism is not the worker's justice, it is his passion: his whim, until it becomes his crucifixion.

This is not just a manner of speaking. The representation of the being-together of equals as a fraternal community can be thought of strictly as a passion of democracy's youth – as democracy acceding to self-consciousness in a universe of oligarchic values. It would be tempting to illustrate this coming to awareness in concrete terms as an existential choice presenting itself to an intelligent and energetic young worker in the days of Louis Philippe: the savings bank versus the community, establishment in the work world versus revolution. But the democratic passion is precisely the possibility of accumulating the choices offered at the crossroads, of being prepared to be torn in all directions at once. The voyage to Icaria was thus a simultaneous departure for the new world of both business and community. From this perspective, the worst is not always inevitable for communists, but it is for community, which in every instance is sure to find equality in a different place or in a different form from the one expected. Community wanted to forge equals through brotherhood. The problem was that it had equals already, in the shape of hybrid beings, mongrels of varied aspect, all of which bear the stamp of inequality: the worker eager to enjoy the fruits of his labour, the smooth-talking orator who is as much at home in the assembly hall as in the tavern, the fraternal beggar playing the exploited philanthropist. Even in his experimental, and for that matter caricatural, form, this mongrel was now the new legislator – the one before whom the old-style legislator, the founder of cities, must bend. This is what Father Cabet learned to his cost: the professor of fraternity was beaten on his own ground – that of speech – by smooth-tongued debaters, and thrown out of his own community. The agency of the law, of the declaration of equality which defined being-in-common, was now in the hands of a character continually involved in excess or default. Perhaps this fable of the professor of equality torn apart by his disciples masks a more secret rending of workers' democracy in its youth?

5. Community and Society: The Paradox of Equality

Should not such teachers of fraternal equality have foreseen this outcome? One person at least had warned them – someone who had been Cabet's professor of Roman law at Dijon, someone of whom many Icarians were avowed followers: Joseph Jacotot, theorist of the equality of intelligence. Twenty years before they set sail for America, Jacotot had seen in the Icarians' minds, as in the minds of all egalitarians, the most radical of challenges to their assumption that the principle of the community of equals and the principle of the social body were one and the same. Equality, he taught, was a belief implied by the very idea of intelligence. Belief in it, acquired or reacquired, was the basis of a community of equals, a community of emancipated men. But such a community did not amount to a society. The notion of *social* equality was a contradiction *in adjecto*. Pursuing it could only contribute to the forgetting of equality itself.

More particularly, Jacotot alerted the egalitarians to the impossibility of binding two contradictory logics: the egalitarian logic implied by the act of speaking and the inegalitarian logic inherent in the social bond. There could never be any coincidence between the two different senses in which the speaking being is prey to arbitrariness: to the arbitrariness of language on the one hand and to the arbitrariness of the social bond on the other.

Let us take the arbitrariness of language to mean simply that there is no reason immanent to language, no divine or universal language, but merely a mass of sounds which it behoves each individual to invest with meaning at each use. This arbitrariness turns both every utterance and every reception into an adventure which presupposes the tense interaction of two wishes: a wish to say and a wish to hear, each threatened at every moment by the danger of falling into the ordinary abyss of distraction, above which is stretched the tightrope of the will to meaning. What this tension presupposes, always provided that it continues to posit it itself, is the virtuality of another tension – the virtuality, that is, of the tension of the other.

The ever-renewed effort exerted by this presupposition may be given a variety of names. Some call it simply reason. Jacotot felt more faithful to its nature and exercise in calling it equality, or rather belief in the equality of intelligences. To speak of the *equality* of intelligences had two basic implications: first, that every spoken or written sentence takes on meaning only if it assumes a subject whose corresponding venture permits the discernment of a meaning the truth of which no pre-existing code or dictionary supplies; and second, that there are no two ways of being intelligent, that every intellectual procedure follows the same path, the path of a materiality traversed by form or meaning, and that the seat of intelligence is always the presupposed equality of a wish to say and a wish to hear.

This is precisely what was implied by Menenius Agrippa's journey to the Aventine hill to tell his fable to the plebeians. Behind that fable's moral, which illustrated the inequality of functions in the social body, lay quite a different moral, one inherent in the very act of composing a fable. This act of composition was based on the assumption that it was necessary to speak and that this speaking would be heard; the assumption of a pre-existing equality between a wish to speak and a wish to hear. Above all, it put this presupposition into practice. The relationship of a representative of the upper class to the members of the lower class was subordinated to a different one, the relationship of narrator to listeners, which is not just an egalitarian relationship but a relationship whose egalitarianism is posited, and should be enhanced, by the storyteller's art itself. The moral of the very act of fabulation was thus the equality of intelligences. And this equality shapes and defines a community, though it must be remembered that this community has no material substance. It is borne at each and every moment by someone for someone else – for a potential infinity of others. It occurs, but it has no place.

Of course the interweaving of the two relationships operates in both directions. Equality must be posited if inequality is to be explained. But the thing that needs explaining, the thing that sets the machine of explanation in motion, is inequality, the absence of reason that must be rationalized, the facticity that has to be put in order, the social arbitrariness that demands the establishment of ranks. In short, the arbitrariness of language that for one rational subject is traversed by another presumes another, social, arbitrariness. All that is meant by social arbitrariness is that the social order is devoid of any immanent reason, that it is merely because it is, without any organizing purpose. In this it seems at first altogether comparable to the arbitrariness of language. But there is a radical and immediately overriding difference: the material arbitrariness of the social weight of things cannot be traversed by any subject for another subject. There is no reasoning collective subject. Only individuals are endowed with reason. A collectivity can have no *wish* to speak to anyone. Society is ordered in the same way as bodies fall to earth. What society asks of us is simply to acquiesce: what it demands is our consent.

What binds us together prior to all community, prior to any equality of intelligence, is the link that runs through all those points where the weight of things in us becomes consent, all those points where acquiescence comes to be loved as inequality and is reflected in the activities of comparing, setting up and explaining ranks. Tradition readily calls this passion; Jacotot preferred to call it inequality, belief in the inequality of intelligences. Existing without reason, inequality has an even greater need to rationalize itself at every moment and in every place. Jacotot gives such rationalization the generic name of 'explanation'. Explanation in this sense is rooted in the necessity to attribute reason to something that has none, to things whose lack of reason is intolerable. In this way, simple non-reason, the contingency of things, is turned into active unreason. And this 'origin of inequality' is reiterated in every explanation; every explanation is a fiction of inequality. I explain a sentence to someone because I assume that he would not understand it if I did not explain it to him. That is to say, I explain to him that if I did not explain he would not understand. I explain to him, in short, that he is less intelligent than I am, and that that is why he deserves to be where he is and I deserve to be where I am. The social bond is maintained by this endless manufacture of acquiescence, which in schools is called explanation and in public assemblies and courts goes by the name of persuasion. Explanation turns all *wishing to say* into a scholar's secret; rhetoric turns all *wishing to hear* into knowing how to hear.

Even before Cabet and the Icarians came to blows over the principles of community – over work versus fraternity – Jacotot conveyed to them the disconcerting message that there was no principle of the community of equals which was also a principle of social organization. There was no *ratio cognoscendi* that was at the same time a *ratio essendi*. There were but two ways of grasping hold of arbitrariness, the primary non-reason of things and of language: the egalitarian reason of the community of equals or the inegalitarian unreason of social bodies. The community of equals can always be realized, but only on two conditions. First, it is not a goal to be reached but a supposition to be posited from the outset and endlessly reposited. All that strategies or pedagogies of the community of equals can do is cause that community to fall into the arena of active unreason, of explanatory/explained inequality ever seeking to pass itself off as the slow road to reconciled futures. The second condition, which is much like the first, may be expressed as follows: the community of equals can never achieve substantial form as a social institution. It is tied to the act of its own verification, which is forever in need of reiteration. No matter how many individuals become emancipated, society can never be emancipated. Equality may be the law of the community, but society inevitably remains in thrall to inequality. Attempting to set up the community of labour or the community of fraternity amounts to casting the imaginary veil of the One over the radical division of the two orders and their inextricable entwinement. A community of equals can never become coextensive with a society of the unequal, but nor can either exist without the other. They are as mutually exclusive in their principles as they are mutually reinforcing in their existence. Anyone proposing to put the principle of their union into practice, to make society equal, should be confronted by the following dilemma: a choice must be made between being equal in an unequal society and being unequal in an 'equal' society, a society which transforms equality into its opposite. A community of equals is an insubstantial community of individuals engaged in the ongoing creation of equality. Anything else paraded under this banner is either a trick, a school or a military unit.[10]

6. The Community of Sharing

Such was the warning that the young fraternal workers had absolutely no wish to hear. Or, to be more precise, in one sense they did not hear it, while in another sense they did – interpreting it after their own fashion. They did not hear it in the sense that they sought to transform the governing idea of community into an organizing concept of social experience. They set themselves up as mentors to the people and martyrs to brotherhood, a posture that old Cabet had adopted long before them. They thus doomed themselves at one stroke to the bitterness of disillusioned teachers and to the indiscipline of unruly students. But their pedagogical and apostolic passion was more than mere unconsciousness, for it rested also on a particular understanding of the fable of the Aventine hill, one which for them meant that the equality of speaking beings could affect social reality. This further displaced the emphasis of the scene, its key moment, not just from the fable's content to the speech situation that produced it, but thence to events that had preceded that context and indeed brought it into being. For Menenius Agrippa to compose his fable, the plebeians had to have withdrawn to the Aventine hill in the first place; they further had to have spoken, to have named themselves, to have made it clear that they were speaking beings whom it was appropriate to approach and address. The egalitarian presupposition, the communal invention of discourse, requires an initial breakthrough which introduces into the community of speaking beings some who were not hitherto of its number. This breakthrough induces a different economy of the presupposition of equality. The effectiveness of the community of speaking beings is predicated on a violence which antedates it. The essence of this inaugurating violence, which has nothing to do with counting dead and wounded, is to make the invisible visible, to give a name to the anonymous and to make words audible where only noise was perceptible before. It creates separation in a community, making room for debate therein, yet it is itself only possible inasmuch as it projects the egalitarian presupposition back into the past. Thus, equality is not simply that presupposition which ascribes social congregation in the last instance to the community of speaking beings, as to a principle necessarily forgotten; for it is manifest in the recurring rupture which, by projecting the egalitarian presupposition back to a point anterior to itself, endows it with social effectiveness. The egalitarian presupposition is not just the immaterial, poetic thread of the community of equals weaving its way through the great fictional fabric of inegalitarian society, for it brings into play social means of verifying equality, that is, means of verifying community within society.

We can understand, therefore, why our young fraternal workers paid no heed to the voice that warned them of the disharmony between the logic of society and the logic of community. The fact was that they themselves had experienced the new ways of verifying the declaration of equality warranted by its reappearance – and revolutionary reinscription – in July 1830. Earlier, I offered an analysis of the tactics of logical demonstration which characterized the transition from the old journeymen's 'damnation' to the modern strike and gave substantial form to the idea of social emancipation. I tried to show how the configuration of material conflict as rational argument took as its core a kind of syllogism imposing an obligation to proceed from the declaration of equality to its effective deployment. By contrasting the fact of the inscription of equality with the facts of actual inequality, this approach successfully replaced dismissal as a groundless claim by its opposite, by a ground for making a claim, a basis for argument, a space for disputation where the relationship between like and unlike could come into play and where the words of equality were genuinely subject to verification. The result was the creation of a community of sharing in both senses of the term: a space presupposing a single, shared rationality, but also a place whose very unity depended on the effecting of a division; a polemical community brought into being to impose a hitherto unacknowledged consequence of the discourse of equality. Whereas Jacotot's critique confined the verification of equality within the continually recreated relationship between a wish to say and a wish to hear, such a verification becomes 'social', causes equality to have a real social effect, only when it mobilizes an *obligation* to hear. The young Jacotist proletarian thus had to clear his own way to the verification of the equality of speaking beings – contributing his own intellectual adventure, as it were, to *Les Aventures de Télémaque*. The equality of speaking beings made itself readable in his experience through a very specific text, to which recourse was unavoidable in that it itself recalled the event of its own inscription and drew its meaning from the act which reactivated that event and carried it beyond itself. At the conjuncture which concerns us the text in question was not so much the Charter as its preamble, not so much the constitutional law as the declaration of the basis of that law, it being understood that this basis itself was rooted in nothing more than the structure of repetition. The declaration repeated the event that had taken place, constituting it as already written, already obligatory. It was itself designed for repetition, and to further whatever repetition was capable of producing by way of new egalitarian events.

So the egalitarian polemic invents an insubstantial community completely determined by the contingency and resolve of its enactment. This egalitarian invention of community refuses the terms of the dilemma that forces a choice between the immateriality of egalitarian communication and the inegalitarian weight of social bodies. Social materiality is not just that weight of bodies to which only the discourse of inegalitarian rationalization applies. For it too may be traversed by a wish-to-say which posits community by presupposing concord in a specific form, the form of an obligation to hear. The *there is* of the event brings out the facticity of *being-there-together*. In the movement of the event replayed, of the text restaged, the community of equals occasionally finds the wherewithal to imprint the surface of the social body with the traces of its actual effects.

The communist passion cannot therefore be reduced to a misinterpretation either of Plato's *Republic* or of the Christians' mystical body; nor can it be reduced to the inability of a youthful workers' democracy to deal with the indeterminacy and boundlessness of its desire. The original source of the communitarian miscalculation lies in a singular experience of transgression. I characterized this transgression earlier, in Platonic terms, as the revolt of cardinal against ordinal, but the revolt in question was a far cry from the Platonic opposition between the arithmetical multiplicity of desires and the geometrical proportionality of the well-ordered community. It was grounded in a logical experience, that of a common measure applied to incommensurables. Equality and inequality are incommensurate with each other, and yet, when the egalitarian event and the invention of community connect, they do indeed become commensurable. The experience of this common measure is an extreme experience. Equality is an exception. Its necessity is governed by the contingency and the resolve which inscribe its presupposition in transgressive strokes lending themselves to the invention of community, to the invention of demonstrations of effective community. It is not hard, then, to understand the attraction, the continually renewed dream, of community as a body united by some principle of life (love, fraternity or work) having currency among the members of that body or serving as a yardstick in the distribution of functions within it. The accepted measuring-rod of the egalitarian exception is the violence which is repeatedly reproduced in response to the tension generated by the vain attempt to suppress it. The practice of the community of sharing in itself nourishes the passion for sharing without dividing, the passion for an equality with substance in a social body which is measured by it. The communist passion yearns to release equality from its exceptionalism, to suppress the ambivalence of sharing, to transform the polemical space of shared meaning into a space of consensus. Beyond any misunderstanding about the idea of the communitarian body, the communist dream of the nineteenth century held firm to the egalitarian experience, to the measurement of the incommensurable, just as Kantian transcendental appearance held firm to the experience of a specific destiny for reason.

Consequently, the satisfaction of having overcome the dead ends and follies of community was in danger of meaning only that the exceptionalism of equality had been forgotten. Beyond communitarian miscalculations lay the appeal of that simple equation which reduces equality to the rule of the principle of unification of the multitude under the common law of the One. With the time of reverence for rhetoric and the glorification of new beginnings safely past, a return would at last be made to that terra firma where justice comes down to the common measure of the *jus*. Yet such a return quickly encounters the necessity that allows the established state to underwrite any kind of communitarian equality only if that state backs it up by projecting all legal-political authority behind it, in the form of the metalegality of the Rights of Man, so that the unresolvable question whether equality is the foundation of community or vice versa has to be addressed at this level. The unresolvable question gives rise to endless argument between the partisans of equality based on the common measure of the universal and the partisans of equality based on respect for the tiniest of differences. This endless argument would be of no consequence were it not for the fact that its very unresolvability serves to justify the practice of submitting every case of the application of equality, as inscribed in the legal-political text, to the wisdom of the legal experts. The trouble is that experts in law exist whereas experts in equality do not – or, more exactly, that equality begins only when the power of the experts ceases to hold sway. Wherever the vaunted triumph of law and of the legal state takes the form of recourse to experts, democracy has been reduced to a caricature of itself – to nothing more than government by wise men.

The memory of the communitarian miscalculation is thus the memory of the fact that equality may be inscribed upon the social body only through the experience of the measurement of incommensurables, through the recollecting of an event that constituted the inscription of the presupposition of equality and through the restaging of that event. Such restaging has no foundation and is justified by a 'there was' which always refers back to yet an earlier 'there was'. The communitarian obligation is bound to the violent contingency of the event and to the facticity of being-there-together. The way in which facticity becomes a principle of obligation is indeed one of the oldest (yet ever fresh) scandals for political thinking, which has never ceased battling with it, whether as enactment or as community. Here we are put in mind, on the one hand, of the way in which Hannah Arendt, in *On Revolution*, confronts the monstrousness whereby some population or other, by virtue merely of geographical chance, is described as a free and equal people, so that qualities which can properly be applied only to an acting subject are ascribed to a state or body. On the other hand, one recalls Aristotle's reflections as he grapples with another aspect of the problem: who should govern? Logic suggests that the best should hold power and exercise it for as long as possible. But Aristotle finds that this ideal cannot always be realized. Specifically, in the case of a city made up of men who are all free and of like nature, the golden rule must give way to facticity. We are confronted by the fact of a city that is a *plethos* – 'a lot of people', all possessing the attribute of freedom. Here, in short, the politician is helpless and can only go along with things as they are until he can somehow find a way to have the justice of proportion prevail amidst the confusion entailed by the rule of the many. Now the characteristic thing about the modern way of founding equality is that it worsens the scandal of facticity and heightens the contingency of the being-there-together of the *plethos* by means of an egalitarian act which is the inscription of the unfoundable right of the multitude.

The invention of community – the ever-to-be-recommended invention of the community of equals – is kindled in the disjointed and random relationship between what is there and what forces change; in the facticity of the process of sharing; and in what it is that causes this process to refer back to an earlier coming together of egalitarian event and egalitarian text. In this way, a particular relationship is established between the invention of community and the state of the social realm. From the invention of community flow a number of effects which eventually come to be inscribed in the social fabric in the shape of hybrid forms that may equally well be described as conquests for the workers, as new means of tightening the bonds of domination or as aspects of the consensual self-regulation of a social machine now going merrily on its way without asking itself any more questions. Such profit-and-loss calculations leave out the essential thing, however, which is that these aspects of the social inscription of invented community constitute a topography, an aleatory distribution of places and cases, of sites and situations, which in their very dispersal are so many opportunities for a resurgence of the egalitarian signifier, for a fresh corroborative delineation of the community of equals. Democracy is not the simple dominion of the common law as inscribed in legal-political texts, nor is it the plural dominion of the passions. It is first and foremost the space of all those locations the facticity of which tallies with the contingency and resolve of the egalitarian inscription in the making. Thus, the street, the factory or the university can become the locus of a resurgence of this kind in response to the chance passage of some apparently insignificant political measure, to a word out of place or an ill-judged assertion, any of which may open the door to a fresh testing of community, to a reinscription of the egalitarian signifier, to the recollection of the earlier event that inscribed itself forcibly in this place. In the autumn of 1986, for instance, we saw how the single word 'selection' had the power to establish a new communication between the egalitarian signifier and the factual situation, existing in France, of a university open to all regardless of economic considerations. Those who at the time contrasted the success of this movement, so circumscribed in its goals and organization, with the vain revolutionary dream of 1968, evidently forgot that the victorious calm of the moment was only possible thanks to the violence of those earlier events which had put the university in question and used the streets to effect communication between the university as a place and society as a whole.

There can therefore be moments of community – not those festive moments that are sometimes described, but dialogic moments, moments when the rule laid down by Gregory of Nazianzus is contravened, when an impertinent dialectic is created by those who have no rights in the matter, but who nevertheless assert such rights in the junction between the violence of a new beginning and the invocation of something already said, something already inscribed. There are moments when the community of equals appears as the ultimate underpinning of the distribution of the institutions and obligations that constitute a society; moments when equals declare themselves as such, though aware that they have no fundamental right to do so save the appeal to what has been inscribed earlier, which their action raises behind it as a banner. They thus experience the *artificial* aspect of their power – in the sense that 'artifice' may mean both something that is not necessary and something that is to be created.

Notes

1   Rom. 12:5; see also 1 Cor. 12:12.

2   Aristotle, *Rhetoric*, III, 1411a, 24.

3   Aristotle, *Politics*, III, 128b, 1–3.

4   See translation of 1 Cor. 12:12 in 'Traditions communistes', *La Fraternité*, December 1842, p. 110.

5   Discours 32, in Grégoire de Nazianze, *Discours 32 à 37*, Paris 1985, pp. 109–11.

6   See also Phil. 2:6, abundantly cited by Marius Victorinus in his *Adversus Arium*. See *Traités théologiques sur la Trinité*, Paris 1960, notably sections 1, 9, 13, 21, etc.

7   Saint Basile, *Lettres*, Paris 1957, vol. 1, p. 54.

8   Saint Basile, *Traité du Saint Esprit*, vol. 1, Paris 1946, pp. 204–6.

9   *Le Populaire*, 21 January 1849.

10   For further thoughts on this, perhaps I may be permitted to direct the reader to my *Le Maître ignorant*, Paris 1987; English translation by Kristin Ross, *The Ignorant Schoolmaster*, Stanford, Calif. 1991.

4

Democracy Corrected

'So, in what was nominally a democracy, power was really in the hands of the first citizen.'[1] In politics, everything depends on certain founding utterances. We still have to decide how such utterances are to be understood. Here, we shall proceed on the hypothesis that Thucydides' famous characterization of the government of Pericles is not 'political' in the sense of reflecting the disillusioned wisdom of one who is used to commanding men and who observes the contradiction between showy phrases and solid realities. The gap between names and things, whose perversions Thucydides well knew, is precisely what defines the space of political rationality. Thus, democracy is not 'just a word' or an illusion. Rather, it is a disposition of the name and appearance of the people, a way of keeping the people present in their absence. Thucydides tells us this: politics is not in the first instance the management of the interests of the community, nor is it the simple art of subduing the populace by means of fine words. It is the apparatus whereby the people are kept within the visible sphere that the people's name rules over: as the subject that occupies the gap between the fiction of community on the one hand and the surfeit of reality of the populace on the other, the people serve both to link and to separate the two, themselves alternately taking on and losing definition as the features of the two intermingle.

1. Disproportionate and Anarchic

My aim in what follows is merely to give resonance to the singularity of Thucydides' words in the faintly anxious satisfaction of our present time, which simultaneously rejoices in the triumph of democracies and wonders whether they are in fact governable. The presumable cynicism of the ancient historian, a friend of the Sophists, would doubtless prompt an amused reaction to the gravity of our queries. Thucydides was well aware that the question of politics was indivisible from that of whether democracies were governable. But he also knew that this question is invariably already settled, that democracies are always both governed and ungovernable – indeed governed inasmuch as they are ungovernable. There is politics, the art and science of politics, because there is democracy. Politics is encountered as already present in the factuality of democracy, in the very strangeness of the combination of words which joins the unassignable quantity of the *demos* to the indefinable action of *kratein*. The primary unsettling factor in this juxtaposition is not that the people are too ignorant for matters which demand knowledge, too fickle for matters which demand stability, too excitable when prudence is called for or too petty when grandeur is required. Rather, it is that the people are always more or less than they are supposed to be: the majority instead of the assembly, the assembly instead of the community, the poor instead of the city, applause instead of agreement, pebbles counted instead of a firm decision taken. Reaching a decision by totting up pebbles and the bemoaning of the stupidity of majorities are the small change of that 'one too many', that divergence from itself, which constitutes the *demos* as such. The people are at once disproportionate and anarchic. Language bears witness to this: there can be no *arche* corresponding to the *demos* as subject, no way of ruling according to some inaugurating principle; there is only a *-cracy* – a manner of prevailing. Prevailing because one is the best, say Pericles' admirers Thucydides and Callicles; prevailing because one prevails, retorts his detractor Plato. The *-cracy* of the best – of the *kreitton* – is no quality, no definable expertise, but rather the sheer extra weight borne by the one best able to submit to the dictates of his own desire, who prevails among the people; for he who gives the people the greatest number of arsenals, the greatest number of colonies and the greatest sense of their own importance, is the one who receives the most power from them in return. The 'one too many' of democracy here allows itself to be reduced to the 'more, always more' of unsatisfied desire, of the economic imperialism that turns democracy into the child of oligarchy and the mother of tyranny.

The concept of politics originated in a choice concerning democracy: whether to declare democracy unworkable as the regime of the dissimilar and entrust the welfare of the city to the philosophical use of speech and the mathematical use of numbers, or, alternatively, to run democracy on the basis of its very dissimilarities, its very ungovernability, using its constitutive self-division for and/or against it: to institute the constitutional rules and customs of government that would allow the people to enjoy the visibility of their power through the dispersal and even delegation of their qualities and prerogatives. The latter approach is exemplified practically in the arrangements (*sophismata*) that are Aristotle's response to the Platonic denunciation of democratic sophistry.

This is the hypothesis of democracy corrected – democracy governed by the judicious use of its own ungovernability. This is not a matter of trickery, or the cynical or penitent juggling of words and things, scenery and props. It is a matter of accomplishing the goal of politics, of leading the community harmoniously through discord itself, through the impossibility of the people being equal to themselves. The triumph of solid facts over showy phrases is also the triumph of the political *logos* over democratic factuality. It is tempting to try and frame the encounter with factuality here in terms of a clearly defined dialectic in which the essence of politics is realized through its own negation. In the first place, there would be the idea of politics, the archetype of which Aristotle outlines in Book I of the *Politics*: community founded on the specifically human power of the *logos*, the power of making manifest the expedient and the harmful, and hence the just and the unjust. In the second place, there would be the pure factuality of the city divided into rich and poor, split not just by fortune but also by the desire for power. And finally, there would be the system of forms and arrangements whereby the political *logos* is realized through its capacity to overcome the twofold division of the people – its difference from itself and its division into classes.

But perhaps, by imposing itself on the factuality of the division of wealth, this dialectic of communitarian reason misses the core of politics – its true 'origin'. For how exactly are we to conceive of that first manifestation of the expedient and harmful which, according to Aristotle, occurs in the course of deliberation upon the just and the unjust? How does the manifestation of the expedient (*to sumpheron* – that which converges, which brings together in a useful way, which serves to bring together) entail the manifestation of the just, of justice as a political principle? The fact is that the *sun* in *sumpheron* does not suffice to differentiate the human city from communities of ants or bees. Heraclitus already knew this: the *logos* is *sumpheromenon/ diapheromenon*. To reach the just from the starting-point of the expedient it is necessary to go by way of opposites, by way of *blaberon/adikon*: 'the harmful and thus the unjust', as the translators often phrase it. But this is to obliterate the very heart of the matter, which is the asymmetry of the *sumpheron* and the *blaberon*. The *blaberon* is not just the harmful or inexpedient: it is that which wrongs or injures. Useful convergence – that earnest pipedream of the so-called liberal age – affects the constitution of the political realm only if it is part of that grievance, that wrong needing righting, which is antithetical to the useful yet not symmetrical with it. The factuality of the division between rich and poor is not the obstacle beyond which the political *logos* should establish itself. Rather, this factuality gives substance to the grievance thanks to which the register of the just becomes accessible to the register of the useful. Democracy denotes this grievance at the same time as it denotes the people's difference from themselves and the power of appearance attaching to the proclamation of the people's name. Politics is a function of the fact of democracy, of the way in which democracy's factuality presents itself in three forms: the *appearance* deployed by the name of the people, the *imparity* of the people when counted and the *grievance* connected with the antagonism between rich and poor. Politics exists, first, because there are names which deploy the sphere of appearance of the people, even if in the process such names are apt to become separated from 'things'; second, because the people are always too numerous or too few compared with the form of their manifestation; and third, because the name of the people is at one and the same time the name of the community and the name of a part of – or rather a split in – the community. The gap between the people as community and the people as division is the site of a fundamental grievance. At the outset, it is not the king but the people who have a double embodiment.

Politics is not a function of the fact that it is useful to assemble, nor of the fact that assemblies are held for the sake of the good management of common business. It is a function of the fact that a wrong exists, an injustice that needs to be addressed. But the political wrong associated with the double embodiment of the people is not a wrong like any other. On the one hand, it cannot be assimilated to the sort of juridical wrong that a court of law can address on the basis of laws or regulations. The irreconcilability of the parties antedates any specific dispute. On the other hand, this irreconcilability is not synonymous with inexpiable war or infinite debt. The evolution of the wrong, which is responsible for the definitive transition from an ordered animal society to a human political community, takes place against the backdrop of that radical otherness which Aristotle exemplified in the figure of the stranger to any city, the man who is either subhuman or superhuman – a monster committed to total war or a divinity beyond the reach of all reciprocity. Somewhere between legal adjudication and infinite indebtedness, between law and religion, political grievance bespeaks an irreconcilability which remains addressable, one which gives rise on the one hand to violent manifestations of otherness and on the other to the peaceful handling of conflict – both excessive in respect of any dialogue between the interests involved, as in respect of any established rule concerning reciprocal rights and duties. In response to the name of the people, subjects emerge who take the wrong in hand, who expose the substance of the irreconcilable grievance while simultaneously beginning the process of addressing it by means of disputation.

Politics exists by virtue of the democratic mobilization of this apparatus of appearance, imparity and grievance. This means that it does not exist simply because power or the state exist.

Factors attributed to political history intermix other mechanisms with the political apparatus proper, mechanisms having to do with the exercise of majesty, the vicarship of the divinity, the command of armies or the management of interests. And wherever the 'end' of the political is proclaimed, what is really targeted is this apparatus of appearance, imparity and grievance. This is the upshot when appearance is lost on account of the universal exhibition of the real, when the grievance I have been describing is swamped by the objectification of common 'problems' and ways to solve them, when imparity is replaced by interminable polling for voting intentions or popularity, along with the equally interminable reckoning of indices of good or bad management of common business. Exhibition in place of appearance, exhaustive counting in place of imparity, consensus in place of grievance – such are the commanding features of the current correction of democracy, a correction which thinks of itself as the end of politics but which might better be called post-democracy. These are the forms of a rationalization of democratic ungovernability whose depletion of all estimates and all images, like its limitless production of laws and articles designed to foresee and regulate all grievances, will surely be stopped dead in its tracks by the sudden emergence of new avatars of the monster and of a merciless divinity.

2. Modern Metapolitics

In the modern age, politics is reborn with the redeployment of the name of the people and of the space of the grievance to which that name gives substance. Those who conceive of politics in terms of the state, as our liberal anti-statists persist in doing, can always teach how the roots of the republican state lie in the formation of the nation-state under the monarchy. So far as politics proper is concerned, however, it is reborn when the sphere of appearance of the people begins regaining ground from the prestige of royal majesty and the trappings of the divine vicarship; when the people reappear as the locus of a division and when this division once again demonstrates, at the heart of the legend of community, the asymmetry between the *sumpheron* and the *blaberon*. It is now that new names are proposed for the people and that new subjects come forward well fitted to exhibit and address the wrong that has been done the people: republicans, democrats and revolutionaries – but also workers or proletarians. It is now too, however, that around the mild reveries of the *sumpheron* bringing an industrious community together there begin to prowl far weightier shadows: the shadow of a sovereign people settling all grievances or the shadow of the body of the oppressed people as the locus of an absolute wrong. Herein lies the singularity of modern politics: even as the apparatus of democratic appearance, democratic grievance and democratic imparity is being redeployed, there emerges in parallel a metapolitics which points up the untenability of that apparatus, its contradictoriness or hypocrisy, its crisis or its end. Modern politics comes into being accompanied by the thought of its own elimination. Something that Aristotle and Thucydides took for granted – that the people were at once part and whole, sovereign and not sovereign – has now become a scandalous notion. It is true that Plato conceptualized an absolute antagonism between the Republic and democracy, opposing a metapolitics or politics of the *arche* to the factuality of democracy. But modern metapolitics burrows into the very heart of politics. It demands that the names used by politics resemble its realities and vice versa. The appearance of the people must be strictly confined to the attributes of sovereignty or the appearance of sovereignty dissolved in favour of the realities of the people as producers. The imparity of democracy, strictly defined as the reign of the majority vote, wavers between the unrepresentability of sovereignty and the incalculability of the wrong done the poor. Either the democratic people must be educated according to republican doctrine or else the republic must be brought back to the truth of the reign of interests. Thus, fragile alliances are sacrificed and clashes begin to occur between the different elements of a democratic apparatus now required to embrace congruence between names and things, truths and appearances. For liberals, the archaic passions associated with the name of the people disturb the prospect of the rule of the *sumpheron* – a convergence of the useful and the just destined to put an end to grievance. On the socialist side, the rights of the producers clash with the names assigned by politics, and class war collides with the fictions of the legal system. It was part of Marx's genius that, in a few as yet unsurpassed texts, he was able to bring to life every element in the theatre of politics and modern metapolitics: the words and togas of ancient politics deployed to liquidate royal majesty; the modern management of warring interests; the marvels of bourgeois industry and the icy waters of egoistic calculation; the critique of the rights of man and the denunciation of the absolute non-right of the proletarian; the mission of the class without qualities and the coming reign of the producers; the withering away of the parasitic state and the dictatorship of the proletariat. Marx also identified the essential drama here, or rather the double drama: the tragedy of the unaddressable wrong played out against the background of the idyll of the generation of justice by the rule of useful production. Marx made democracy's separation from itself into the separation of the political realm from itself, giving the split a name that would be adopted by the whole of modernity – and even turned against Marx himself. The name in question was 'ideology'. This was not just a new name for an old idea – illusion, simulacrum or something of the sort – but rather a name for the continually incriminated distance between names and things, the conceptual operator that controls junctions and disjunctions between components of the modern political apparatus. 'Ideology' is what makes it possible in turn to reduce the appearance of the people to the level of an illusion masking real conflict or, conversely, to denounce the names of the people and the manifestations of the people's grievance as anachronisms merely holding up the advent of the rule of the common interest. 'Ideology' links the production of the political sphere to its evacuation, for it designates the gap between words and things as a disturbance *in* politics that may at any time become a disturbance *of* politics. It is an ever-shiftable term which, by rearranging at will the relationships of the people's appearance and grievance, permits the locus of the political to be continually changed – changed, indeed, to the limit, which is the declaration of the end of politics. The 'end of the political' designates the completion of the process whereby the metapolitical, coiled at the heart of the political, eviscerates it from within, and in the name of the critique of appearances so thoroughly erases all mediation of the wrong and injustice done that political justice is reduced to nothing more than the reasonable rule of the *sumpheron*.

3. Racism: The Disease of Consensus

The hypothesis of consensual democracy runs roughly as follows. We are at the end of the time when the appearance of the people and the grievance of the people held sway. We are leaving that period behind: first, on account of the collapse of the 'workers' states', and second, by virtue of the energy with which we have developed and shared our wealth and multiplied individual satisfactions and forms of collective consultation. We can now deal with division for what it has become, namely competition, a form of that convergence thanks to which the production of the useful realizes itself through the production of justice. We can endow the reality of democracy with what we have taken away from its shadow, freeing imparity from the trappings of appearance and the exaggerations of grievance. The present failings of representation, the gap between the parliamentary majority and either the sovereign people or the multiplicity of citizens – and for that matter the absence of any majority, and empty benches in the National Assembly – can be rectified by mechanisms for profiling the people or portions of the people, as by mechanisms designed to objectify problems and solutions, along with the rules for their discussion, in the most exhaustive way. Mechanisms, too, for harmonizing the computation of the parts with the image of the whole in the context of that perpetual overall computation which displays public opinion in its entirety as synonymous with the people as a body. And mechanisms for problematizing any object of grievance liable to revive the name of the people and the appearance of the people's self-division. A grievance is simply the symptom of a problem, and no problem is anything more than the lack of the means to solve it. Exposure of wrong must now give way to identification of the lack, followed by its remedy. This may be a lack of resources to be shared or a lack of rules for the prevention of conflict: the answer to the one is unlimited economic growth, to the other a proliferation of laws and regulations. The exhaustive enumeration of problems to be solved and lacks to be answered calls for a correspondingly precise enumeration of the participants necessary and sufficient to discuss and resolve each case. The image of the round-table discussion appropriate to the problem to hand here contrasts sharply in its completeness with empty parliamentary benches, and it may readily be identified with the hundred per cent of the population polled daily on their desires and choices and displayed broken down into their precise divisions. The objectivity of problems and the enlistment of the contributors needed to solve them thus entails a concurrence of opinions around the solution that offers itself of its own accord as the only one that makes sense.

In this way, politics assigns itself an edifying purpose. Stripped of its theatrical fancy dress, democracy is introduced into this programme as that dialogue, that collective search for *homonoia*, which Plato counterposed to the seductions of rhetoric as the noise of assemblies to popular theatres. But Plato will not accept payment in such cheap coin. For him, the difference between dialogue and rhetorical persuasion cannot define any conceivable correction of democracy. Rather, it defines philosophy's radical difference from democracy. Democracy cannot be redeemed by philosophy. And it is most certainly farcical to posit its dialogic redemption through discussion of the more and the less or the weighing of interests in the balance. Imparity is an essential part of democracy. The only kind of dialogue compatible with democracy is one where the parties hear one another but do not agree with one another, the kind of dialogue which takes place on the stage. Democracy is closely linked to tragedy – to unsettled grievance. The modern experience of democracy has refuted the over-simple Platonic identification of democratic imparity with the masses' desire for 'more, always more'. But at least it has confirmed Plato's intuition: democracy is not the search for *homonoia* – and especially not the fairy tale which clothes the debating of common interests in the garb of philosophical dialogue. Democratic dialogue in this respect resembles poetic dialogue as defined by Mandelstam: the interlocutor is indispensable to it, but so is the indeterminacy of that interlocutor – the unexpectedness of his countenance.[2] Democratic dialogue refuses the objectification implied by 'partnerships' and their 'problems'. An interlocutor is not a 'partner'. And the advances of democracy have always been due to improvisation by unprogrammed actors, by surplus interlocutors: a noisy crowd occupying the street, a silent crowd crossing their arms in a factory and so forth. We are talking here not about spontaneous action by the people but about democratic imparity. No 'wildcatting' against the organization is involved, for such improvised crowds have always been able quickly to provide themselves with representatives to go and parley in civil fashion with the spokespeople of wealth and power whenever the latter were willing and ready to receive them. The political wrong, as we have seen, can be addressed. But addressed does not mean redressed. To assume that a common language and a comprehension by each side of the other's reasoning are prerequisites for the wrong's being made manifest and being debated is not the same thing as objectifying that wrong as a problem whose solution is sought by partners acting together. The parties in confrontation do not make up any whole capable of definitively righting the wrong. The subject that gives voice and substance to the grievance is not qualified to declare it satisfied. Nor is there any justification for setting up an opposition, as Habermas does, between the discursive formation of a will to democracy and liberal compromise between interests. Democracy is neither compromise between interests nor the formation of a common will. Its kind of dialogue is that of a divided community. Not that it is indifferent to the universal, but in politics the universal is always subject to dispute. The political wrong does not get righted. It is addressed as something irreconcilable within a community that is always unstable and heterogeneous. This is also why there is no reason to counterpose a postmodern logic of the explosion of language games and the heterogeneity of the *différend* to the modern logic of grievance founded on the common language of the wrong, the great narrative of the people and the display of the universal victim.[3] For one thing, the place of the wrong in the framework of politics is prior and indeed constitutive relative to any figuration of the universal victim, so the eclipse of the one does not entail the nonexistence of the other. The political metamorphoses of the people and their grievance cannot be reduced to this metapolitical figuration. Also, the homogeneity of the proletarian grievance and of the proletarian narrative does not stand in simple opposition to the multiplicity of language games. The realm of grievance is not in fact a homogeneous one, while the great proletarian narrative is epitomized by a multitude of minor language games and minor grievances, a plethora of instantiations and scenarios of the wrong which are always played out at the frontier between homogeneity and heterogeneity, systematically mixing up different levels of speech and refusing community even as they constitute it. Grievance is the true measure of otherness, the thing that unites interlocutors while simultaneously keeping them at a distance from each other. Here again what Mandelstam says about poetic interlocution may be applied to politics: it is not a question of acoustics but of distance. It is otherness which gives meaning to language games, not the other way round. Likewise, dreams of a new politics based on a restricted and generalized otherness, on multiform networks redirecting the flows of the communication and information machine, have had only disappointing results, as we well know. Unless it is religious, otherness can only be political, that is, founded on a wrong at once irreconcilable and addressable. When the apparatus of grievance disappears, what takes over in its stead is simply the platitude of consensus, which does not take long to reveal to those of a realist bent, who are so delighted to see the people's political passions soothed, its inevitable dark side: the return to the political animal state – and the pure and simple rejection of the other.

Testimony to this is supplied us every day in the form of pathetically well-intentioned consensual round tables aiming to solve the problems of which current outbreaks of racism are said to be just symptoms. The trouble is that racism is not the symptom but the disease – the disease, in fact, of consensus itself, the loss of any measure of otherness. The transmogrification of the other to the frenzied point of pure racist rejection and the erasure of the other through the problematization of immigration are two sides of the same coin. It is the 'sensible' supplanting of appearance by exhibition, of imparity by counting and of grievance by consensus that invites the monster back to where the political now fails to reach. It is the exhaustive counting of a population forever being polled that replaces the people (now declared an anachronism) by the subject referred to as 'The French', a subject whose first manifestation – on a par with the latest apodictic political forecasts by some junior minister – is liable to be some very emphatic opinions on the excessive number of foreigners, the feebleness of the government's repressive measures or the shockingly soft life led by prison inmates. It is the regime of universal exhibition and the attendant promise of the total realization of all fantasies (for the paltry cost of a Minitel connection) which ensconce, at the very centre of the parade of desirable objects, the figure of the thwarter of wholesale enjoyment. And it is the dissolution of the subject of grievance which creates a wordless victim, object of an unquenchable hatred. The immigrant is first and foremost a worker who has lost his name, a worker who is no longer perceptible as such. Instead of the worker or proletarian who is the object of an acknowledged wrong and a subject who vents his grievance in struggle and disputation, the immigrant appears as at once the perpetrator of an inexpiable wrong and the cause of a problem calling for the round-table treatment. Alternately problematized and hated, the immigrant is caught in a circle, one might even say a spiral: the spiral of lost political otherness, doomed to the unnameable form of hatred that goes hand in hand with the realists' wish to rid problems of 'emotions'. There is no way of taking passion out of politics. There is the passion for equality and the passion for inequality, as the ingenuous or cynical responses of respectable round-table participants clearly show: it is all right to debate racism if you first give way on equality, or to give the other the run of the city so long as he is denied citizenship a priori.

Depoliticizing conflicts in order to settle them, or stripping otherness of any yardstick the better to solve its problems – this is the madness which our time identifies with a reasonable and easy democracy that harmonizes state initiatives with the natural tendencies of productive society, with its efforts and desires.[4] The state, we are told, must be modest, restoring or leaving to society its dynamism and ability to guarantee the harmonious coexistence of its agents. For this the state must be socialized in the right way, must get itself in tune with the hum of the world's energies, with the rhythms of the production and circulation of things, people and information, by adopting the same modes of management, communication and consultation as the business enterprise. Unfortunately, for the state to be modest, society also would have to be modest. The one is never more nor less modest than the other. They simply take turns at being the one to display the immodesty of both, and, at the moment, it happens to be society's turn to display immodesty, to identify itself with the permanent promise of everything to everyone, which is to say the permanent frustration of everyone in everything. The great metapolitical illusion of modernity is precisely this antagonism between a modest society and an immodest state, an antagonism within whose terms liberals and socialists have never ceased to commune. The cold monster of the state has never ceased working for the hot monster of society, for all the desirable objects that society exhibits as critics of appearance and felicitous resolutions of otherness. State and society enter into opposition with each other, in fact, only with the falling into oblivion of politics – with the abandonment of the fundamental relationship of the principled character of politics to the factuality of democracy, to the apparatus of appearance, imparity and grievance. Society no more holds the solution to the state's problems than the state holds the solution to social problems. The folly of the times is the wish to use consensus to cure the diseases of consensus. What we must do instead is repoliticize conflicts so that they can be addressed, restore names to the people and give politics back its former visibility in the handling of problems and resources.

Notes

1   Thucydides, *History of the Peloponnesian War*, trans. Rex Warner, revised edition, Harmondsworth 1972, II, 65.

2   See Osip Mandelstam, 'O sobesednike' (On the Interlocutor); French translation, 'De l'interlocuteur', in *De la poésie*, Paris 1990.

3   See Jean-François Lyotard, *La Condition postmoderne*, Paris 1979; English translation by Geoffrey Bennington and B. Massumi, *The Postmodern Condition*, Manchester 1984.

4   See Michel Crozier, *Etat moderne, Etat modeste*, Paris 1987.